NEW DIRECTIONS FOR STUDENT SERVICES

Margaret J. Barr, *Texas Christian University*
EDITOR-IN-CHIEF

M. Lee Upcraft, *The Pennsylvania State University*
ASSOCIATE EDITOR

Racism on Campus: Confronting Racial Bias Through Peer Interventions

Jon C. Dalton
Florida State University

EDITOR

Number 56, Winter 1991

JOSSEY-BASS INC., PUBLISHERS, San Francisco

MAXWELL MACMILLAN INTERNATIONAL PUBLISHING GROUP
New York • Oxford • Singapore • Sydney • Toronto

RACISM ON CAMPUS: CONFRONTING RACIAL BIAS
THROUGH PEER INTERVENTIONS
Jon C. Dalton (ed.)
New Directions for Student Services, no. 56
Margaret J. Barr, Editor-in-Chief
M. Lee Upcraft, Associate Editor

Microfilm copies of issues and articles are available in 16mm and 35mm,
as well as microfiche in 105mm, through University Microfilms Inc., 300
North Zeeb Road, Ann Arbor, Michigan 48106.

LC 85-644751   ISSN 0164-7970   ISBN 1-55542-780-4

NEW DIRECTIONS FOR STUDENT SERVICES is part of The Jossey-Bass
Higher and Adult Education Series and is published quarterly by Jossey-
Bass Inc., Publishers, 350 Sansome Street, San Francisco, California
94104-1310 (publication number USPS 449-070). Second-class postage
paid at San Francisco, California, and at additional mailing offices. POST-
MASTER: Send address changes to New Directions for Student Services,
Jossey-Bass Inc., Publishers, 350 Sansome Street, San Francisco, Califor-
nia 94104-1310.

SUBSCRIPTIONS for 1991 cost $45.00 for individuals and $60.00 for institutions, agencies, and libraries.

EDITORIAL CORRESPONDENCE should be sent to the Editor-in-Chief,
Margaret J. Barr, Sadler Hall, Texas Christian University, Fort Worth,
Texas 76129.

Cover photograph by Wernher Krutein/PHOTOVAULT © 1990.

Printed on acid-free paper in the United States of America.

CONTENTS

Editor's Notes

Acts revealing racial or ethnic bias that are committed by college students are troubling indicators of the failure to educate our youth to live in a pluralistic community. The qualities of tolerance and an appreciation of differences are not only necessary for a just and humane community but they are also essential for the full development of students as mature individuals.

There are few places so well equipped to educate for diversity as colleges and universities and few times in life when individuals are as open to new experiences and change as during the college years. It is true that colleges and universities cannot be expected to change quickly student attitudes and behaviors about race and ethnicity that are based on a lifetime of influences from peers, family, and popular culture. But educators can be more committed to teaching about diversity and to fostering conditions on campus that will facilitate the development of tolerance and an appreciation of differences.

Much has been written in response to the recent increase in bias-related incidents on predominantly white college campuses. This literature has focused primarily on documenting the incidents, offering administrative strategies for responding to them, and critiquing institutional support programs and services for minority students. Relatively little attention has been given to examining ways in which the leadership and influence of students' peers can be enhanced as a powerful strategy for confronting campus bias. It is our conviction that students themselves can be highly effective educators and role models in efforts to reduce bias and promote an appreciation of differences.

The focus of this volume is on these students—what we know about the roots and causes of bias in them and in their peer environment and how peer leadership can be strengthened to combat expressions of bias in college students' attitudes and behaviors. Eliminating bias and intolerance in college students is inextricably linked to fostering the development of tolerance and an appreciation of differences. Student peers can play an important role in these endeavors when they have support and collaboration from educators and administrators. Peer culture and peer leaders, which exert the most influence on the values and behaviors of college students, can be obstacles in educators' efforts to eliminate bias and promote tolerance, or they can be powerful allies in these endeavors. This volume provides information and strategies that will help make peer leaders into allies in promoting tolerance.

In Chapter One, I provide an overview of recent bias-related incidents on campus and explore the changes in college student values that have contributed to an increase in racial bias and harassment.

In Chapter Two, Donna M. Bourassa offers suggestions on program interventions aimed at three distinct audiences: white students, students of color, and integrated student groups.

In Chapter Three, Shanette M. Harris and Michael T. Nettles investigate how precollege characteristics and college experiences affect the performance and satisfaction of African-American and white students.

In Chapter Four, Cherie R. Brown and George J. Mazza provide bias-reduction strategies based on a successful peer training model.

In Chapter Five, Barbara A. Mann and Rita M. Moser present a theoretical framework to suggest ways of designing interventions to promote appreciation of differences and also examine some existing programs on college campuses.

In Chapter Six, Margaret A. Healy, Diane L. Cooper, and Elaine C. Fygetakis discuss practical approaches to assist student services professionals with the evaluation of peer intervention programs.

The last chapter provides a detailed cross-section of some of the most current and helpful literature on the topic, as compiled by Roberta Christie and Renée Borns.

Incidents of bias and intolerance in college student behavior vary greatly according to the type and size of higher education institution. Since the majority of recent campus bias-related incidents have occurred on predominantly white campuses, we focus our attention on these types of institutions and the special circumstances that typify these student life environments.

We also want to alert the reader to our selection of terms in our discussion of racial and ethnic groups. We use *white* to refer to those students of primarily European descent who usually comprise the majority racial group in the campus environments we discuss. We use *people of color* to refer to all students who represent nonwhite races and ethnic groups on campus. We use this term because it is less stigmatized than others in social usage and is more inclusive. We use *African American* to refer to students of African ancestry. We acknowledge certain problems and limitations with the selection of these particular terms, but after much review, they seem to be the most fitting for our purposes. Of no small consideration was our desire to use terms that are preferred by those to whom they refer.

Finally, I want to express deep appreciation to Maedea Davis whose name does not appear in the list of authors but whose work on this volume was invaluable.

Jon C. Dalton
Editor

Jon C. Dalton is vice president for student affairs and associate professor of higher education at Florida State University.

Campus bias-related incidents are predictable outcomes of increasingly self-interested values and limited personal experience with racial and ethnic diversity.

Racial and Ethnic Backlash in College Peer Culture

Jon C. Dalton

The reemergence of problems based on bias and intolerance among college students during the late 1980s took almost everyone in higher education by surprise. Yet few developments in college student behavior could have been so easily predicted. The outbreak of racial and ethnic hostility on college campuses was the inevitable culmination of fundamental changes in the values of college students, increased competition and stress in higher education, a lack of sufficient personal experience and knowledge among students about racial and cultural diversity, and a societal shift away from concerns about civil rights and social justice to interest in issues of individual rights and consumerism. This chapter examines recent campus incidents of racial and ethnic hostility and the factors that have helped to precipitate them. Contemporary student values and attitudes are also explored to determine the impact they have had on bias-related incidents on campus.

Bias-Related Incidents on Campus

The outbreak of racial and ethnic conflict on campus has produced some of the most serious campus unrest since the Vietnam War. Incidents involving bias and intolerance on campuses across the country have grown quickly into a phenomenon that educators have been powerless to stop. Bias-related incidents have been widely reported in the media, examined in articles and reports, and discussed at numerous educational conferences. These incidents have gained national attention because of the meanness of such acts as cross burnings, verbal and physical intimidation, racial slurs, and the use of degrading and insensitive stereotypes. The National Institute Against Prejudice and Violence (Shenk, 1990) claims that more than 250 colleges have reported racial incidents since the fall of 1986. The Anti-Defamation League of B'nai B'rith (Shenk, 1990) reports a sixfold increase in anti-Semitic episodes on campuses between 1985 and 1988. In 1989 alone the league determined that there were 1,432 anti-Semitic incidents at institutions throughout the country (Dubin, 1990).

Bias-related incidents are not new on college campuses. A decade ago Beckham (1981) conducted a survey of 160 colleges and universities and reported a pattern of increased bias-related incidents. What has alarmed educators in recent years has been the dramatic escalation in the frequency and severity of these incidents. Hively's (1990) report, based on responses from presidents of the 375-member American Association of State Colleges and Universities, contends that intolerance is spreading and will lead to violent clashes on campus unless discriminatory behavior is eliminated. In 1989, racial incidents were reported on 115 American college campuses (Goleman, 1990). Such acts appear to reflect a pattern of college student behavior that will not quickly dissipate.

At the same time, there is considerable disagreement about the causes of the problem and its meaning. A common reaction among educators has been to view the incidents as obvious signs of a resurgent racism among college students. Certainly, the frequency and severity of such incidents provide compelling evidence of a troubling change in the mood and values of white college students. In a national survey of college and university presidents (Boyer, 1990), one in four report racial tensions to be on the rise and racial and ethnic divisions to be deepening on their campuses.

Bias-related incidents may seem more frequent because people of color are more organized and active on campuses and more assertive in bringing complaints to the attention of college administrators. A more aggressive reporting of these incidents may actually reflect a more open and supportive environment for minority students. On the other hand, Shaw (1990) points out that institutions that take positive action to eliminate campus discrimination have no assurance of a conflict-free campus. In fact, he argues, such institutions may experience greater controversy and backlash because of their initiatives. Consequently, institutions that attempt to be responsible and actively address problems of campus bias may even become the most likely targets of protests from people of color.

Despite the debate over why racial incidents are increasing among college students, there seems little doubt that the social mood of these students has changed. Racial and ethnic differences are more openly challenged and confronted now than ever before, and college students frequently fragment into openly hostile camps.

Key Factors in Bias-Related Incidents

In examining the types of racial incidents that have occurred on college campuses, we can isolate several important factors that help to account for these incidents.

White Students' Lack of Knowledge and Experience with People of Color and Their Cultures. Ikenberry (1988) observed that traditional-age college students now know less than they should about the cultures of people of color and do not possess the civility or sensitivity that is necessary to live in a pluralistic society. Today's eighteen- to twenty-two-year-old college students were born after the civil rights era and have little direct knowledge of the struggles of that period. As we shall examine later, most white college undergraduates have limited contact with other people of color prior to college enrollment. Moreover, many white students bring negative racial stereotypes with them to college, particularly of African American students. Muir (1989) reports that in 1988 from 17 to 30 percent of whites in his study still perceived African Americans as incapable, lazy, untrustworthy, and unambitious.

Peer Group Influence. Research (Goleman, 1990) indicates that bias-related crimes are most often committed by youths, especially those in their teens and twenties. A large majority of bias-related incidents are instigated by groups of four or more people. For those individuals, such behavior is often associated with feelings of strong group identity and the instinct to defend or promote the values of the group. The group nature of bias-related incidents is particularly characteristic of such incidents in the college setting, where peer group influence is especially powerful.

Because eighteen- to twenty-two-year-old college students typically struggle with such developmental tasks as forming an identity, establishing independence, and clarifying values, they are likely to adopt behaviors promoted by their peer group, especially if such behaviors reflect values learned from family members. Newcomb and Wilson's (1966) research on peer groups in the college setting clearly documents the powerful influence of group behavior on college students. To understand the root causes of bias-related incidents in the college setting, one must understand the phenomenon of social bonding among college students.

Increased Competition and Stress. College life has become increasingly stressful and competitive for students. Tougher admissions standards, higher costs and fewer financial aid resources, and increasing numbers of limited-access programs have put the squeeze on most college students. Astin (1988) documents the negative effects of such stress on the emotional health of college students. The increased competition and stress felt by white students are fueling backlash behavior toward people of color, who are perceived as having special privileges. As competition for college admission, financial aid, majors, graduate schools, and status jobs has increased, so have white students' feelings of anger and resentment toward people of color.

High Coincidence of Alcohol Use. A common factor in campus bias-related incidents has been the use and abuse of alcohol. In a majority of recent campus incidents, alcohol use was either directly or indirectly related to the events that occurred. Consequently, we must consider the role and significance of alcohol use in college peer culture if we wish to understand why racial incidents have occurred and what can be done to address the problem.

Alcohol use and abuse have long been important factors in behavior problems among college students. There is a high correlation of alcohol use with such problems as vandalism, assault, theft, and the rise of sexually transmitted diseases on campus. Sherrill and Siegel (1989) report that almost half the incidents of campus vandalism are linked to alcohol abuse. Recent alcohol use research (Johnston, O'Malley, and Bachman, 1988) indicates that more than 90 percent of college students report they use alcohol. The fact that alcohol use appears to be so common in bias-related incidents suggests that alcohol plays an important role in lowering inhibitions and impeding responsible decision making.

Protection of Turf or Territory. Goleman (1990) reports that the majority of bias crimes involved issues of "turf" in which individuals were attacked or harassed because they were perceived to be invading someone else's domain. This phenomenon is clearly reflected in urban bias-related crimes in which "outsiders" are attacked for trespassing in ethnically or racially homogeneous neighborhoods.

In the highly congested milieu of most colleges and universities, there may be less guarding of actual physical space, but there are real social and psychological boundaries that separate students and that can result in powerful confrontations when violated. Some typical conflict areas in the college setting include relations between athletes and fraternity members, between African American fraternity and sorority members and their white counterparts, between students living in residence halls and those in fraternities, and between students and nonstudents. In addition, the use of a certain physical space on campus may become identified with a particular student group through custom and practice, and those who do not belong to the group may be unwelcome in that space.

Influence of Off-Campus Groups. There is evidence that off-campus groups are targeting the college campus for dissemination of racist and anti-Semitic literature. Nationally distributed pamphlets, fliers, and newspapers that advocate white supremacy and anti-Semitism are being circulated on many college campuses. There is little available evidence that such attempts are widespread or coordinated, but the heightened sensitivity of race relations on campus and the considerable media attention given to these issues make the college campus vulnerable to external hate mongering.

Perception of Unfair Treatment. Few circumstances seem to provoke intergroup conflict as quickly as the perception that an individual (or group) has been unfairly treated because of his or her racial or ethnic identity. As we have already noted, such issues now come up more frequently on campus because people of color have recently become more assertive of their rights and are more vocal and organized.

What makes the campus scene so volatile today, however, is the fact that white students have also become more militant about what they perceive as unfair treatment. "White backlash" is perhaps best illustrated by the appearance of a new type of student organization called the "white student union." White student unions have appeared on several campuses, and organizers claim that their central purpose is to advocate equal rights for white students who have been excluded from special support programs and other forms of aid and assistance provided by colleges and universities.

White student unions have thus far been more a creation of the media than a significant student movement, yet they may represent a symbolic action taken by a few white students but supported in spirit by many. Wherever they appear, they have been and will continue to be a divisive phenomenon on campus. To people of color they epitomize a new form of blatant racism. College administrators, in turn, will have difficulty controlling the negative fallout from such groups since the right to organize and the right to free speech cannot be prohibited. Thus, these groups exacerbate racial and ethnic tensions and will be a divisive influence in institutional efforts to promote sensitivity and tolerance among students.

Coverage of People of Color in Campus Media. Few things have the potential to provoke students as much as the treatment they receive by the campus press. This is especially true for people of color. On the one hand, concern is often expressed that the campus press simply ignores people of color and their activities. On the other, when there is coverage, it is often negative or incomplete. Terrell (O'Brien, 1990) believes that derogatory remarks are often printed in student newspapers under the guise of freedom of speech. In most large institutions, the student newspaper, radio, and television stations are the primary sources for students of information about the campus. As such, the student media convey what is perceived to be important in the university environment. When there is little attention to minorities in the student newspaper or when the coverage is perceived to be biased or insensitive, it can have a significant influence on students' attitudes toward those who are different from themselves.

Treatment of Minorities by Campus and Community Law Enforcement. Students of color frequently complain about the manner in which they are treated by campus police and local law enforcement officers. Complaints about unnecessary stop-and-search procedures on campus and in off-campus neighborhoods—particularly when those incidents involve African American males—are frequently heard. For many students of color, routine encounters with police are viewed as one of the most negative aspects of the college environment.

Several factors may serve to make relations between police and students of color especially volatile in the campus setting. First, the increase in campus crime in recent years has prompted more aggressive police surveillance on campus. The increased presence and activity of campus and community police in the college environment may be perceived as selective enforcement directed toward people of color. Second, many campus police officers come directly from police academy programs that train them for urban duty and do not prepare them to work on the college campus. Third, college students who come from urban environments often bring with them negative experiences and perceptions about police. These perceptions and attitudes can play an important role in how they interpret encounters with campus and community police. Much of the contact students have with campus police officers is after dark in isolated settings where there may be some element of suspicion and fear. Such encounters can become immediately volatile if not handled with great professionalism by police officers.

College Student Values, Experiences, and Development

The increase in bias-related incidents among college students must also be seen in the context of some fundamental changes in these students' values and experiences and of their struggle with developmental tasks. Efforts to address bias-related incidents on campus must take these changes into consideration if interventions are to be effective.

Changes in Values. The development of self-interested values during the 1970s and 1980s was one of the most remarkable shifts in the beliefs and values of college students to take place during the twentieth century. For almost twenty years, an unbroken trend of increasing concern about money and status was reflected in the beliefs and values of incoming college freshmen (Astin, 1988). This longitudinal research on college freshmen norms clearly documents students' increasing materialism and corresponding decline in concern about social problems, the welfare of others, and the improvement of society. This transformation of student values was no doubt shaped by a national culture in which self-interest and materialism were highly prized (Gelman, 1990). Bok (Radin, 1990) asserts that "there is disturbing evidence to suggest that most forms of responsibility toward others have eroded in recent decades" (p. 11). Buffington (1990) claims that the decade of the 1980s was a decade of greed that left behind a powerful by-product of suspicion. He writes, "Simply, greed incites suspicion, and the problematic thoughts and feelings which result are alive, well, and growing" (p. 102).

While college administrators closely observed this remarkable transformation in students' social consciousness, their focus was primarily on the implications of these value changes for recruitment, retention, program access, and consumer issues on campus. Remarkably little attention has been given to the human relations implications of a generation of college students who now give less priority to social justice issues than to self-interest in their worldview. Today campus incidents based on bias and intolerance and directed at African Americans, Hispanics, Asian Americans, Jews, and other minority groups are the predictable outcomes of a new set of beliefs and values among youth that depreciates the relative worth of other people and their needs. The shift in college student values toward self-interested individualism is directly linked to an increase in intolerant social behavior.

Limited Contact with Other Races and Ethnic Groups. During the seventies and eighties, not only were the values of college students becoming less other-directed but their personal encounters with diverse people and ideas were also becoming more constricted. For college students of the past two decades, the civil rights movement became increasingly remote and unrelated to their own lives. Moreover, there was little in the experience of most new college students that would help to personalize the issues of racial equality and social justice. Ascher (1990) found that prior to college most white students had little opportunity to interact as equals with people of color. Louis (1986) found that many students entering college had never had contact with peers from another racial group. Pace (1990) reports that less than half of all undergraduates make friends with someone of a different race, and even fewer have had a serious discussion about race relations.

Fear of Diversity. Most freshmen bring with them into the college environment some measure of fear and uncertainty about diversity. This characteristic is a reflection of their developmental stage as well as of their limited social experience. In *Forms of Intellectual and Ethical Development in College Students,* Perry (1968) argues that one of the central challenges for students during the college years is to confront diversity and pluralism. Traditional-age students typically come to college with a monolithic worldview in which right and wrong are clearly staked out. As Perry argues, the security of this ordered worldview is shattered as students learn that truth is not so neatly packaged and that there can be multiple viewpoints on even the most fundamental values, beliefs, and so-called facts.

Just as the encounter with intellectual diversity and pluralism is threatening to the new student, so is the social encounter with racial and ethnic diversity. Although one is cognitive and the other is social, these two transitions to college life are arguably the toughest that students must make. Furthermore, they are not unrelated. Some of the mechanisms for coping seem almost identical. The typical student's reaction to intellectual multiplicity is one of high anxiety, complaint, and resentment. As Perry notes, students do not like having their compartmentalized intellectual universe dismantled.

College students often react in much the same way to social encounters with those who are different. They are anxious about social contacts and uneasy about close personal interactions. They are uncertain about how to communicate and resentful of what they view as special or favored treatment. Perry (1968) claims that the threat of multiplicity can be so intimidating to some students that they become what he calls "dedicated reactionaries" (p. 184). They become so convinced of the correctness of their own worldview that they hate those who believe differently. They deal with diversity by simply denying it or refusing to give it any credence—or, at the worst, by attacking it as something evil.

In short, these are some of the circumstances and conditions that influence white students in particular before they reach the college campus: a values hierarchy that gives low priority to understanding and caring for others, little contact and experience with those of racial and ethnic backgrounds different from their own, and fear of intellectual and social diversity.

The Campus Peer Culture

For reasons we are only now beginning to understand, the campus peer culture is perceived by whites as more permissive than in the past of attitudes and behaviors of bias and intolerance. U.S. Representative Walter Fauntroy (1988) claims that there exists today "a new meanness in racial attitudes, as though the internal brakes were off." He argues that white students perceive that it is more permissible now to express racial bias and that such attitudes and behaviors are tacitly, if not openly, endorsed by others. This is evident in the fact that so many racial incidents on campus have occurred publicly, such as telling racially offensive jokes on the campus radio station, sponsoring slave auction parties, and doing skits in blackface. These are not anonymous acts done under the cover of night. Some of them occur out of sheer ignorance, no doubt. Some of them represent deliberate meanness. Most are a mixture of the two. But underlying such behavior is a perception, not always recognized but still there, that this behavior is really not so bad.

Most traditional-age college students must make some adjustments as they encounter the racial and cultural diversity on campus today. It is generally less of an adjustment for African Americans, Hispanics, and Asian Americans because they have had to learn early how to live in a multicultural world. But white students often come to college with some deeply entrenched racial and ethnic stereotypes that reflect learned values from home, peers, and society.

College students are isolated socially; there are few campus settings in which whites and students of color can engage in dialogue about interracial issues. Whiteley and Loxley (1986) found that white freshmen in their Sierra Project had been taught not to mention race for fear that it would create tension and disruption. Thus, students rarely talk about race outside their own ethnic group. In fact, one of the common complaints voiced by administrators when dealing with acts based on bias and intolerance is how hard it is to identity settings where issues between whites and people of color can be shared and discussed. As we shall see in later chapters, one of the most important strategies for addressing bias-related incidents is to create more opportunities for contact and interaction among different racial and ethnic groups on campus.

In order to understand the causes of bias-related incidents in college peer culture and learn how to facilitate peer leadership in addressing this problem, we must know more about how college students relate across racial and cultural boundaries and how they view racial and ethnic differences. Donna Bourassa examines these issues in Chapter Two.

References

Ascher, C. "Ensuring a Rainbow After the Storm: Recent Initiatives to Institutionalize Pluralism on Predominantly White Campuses." *Higher Education Extension Review,* 1990, 2 (1).

Astin, A. W. *The American Freshman: National Norms for Fall 1988.* Los Angeles: Cooperative Institutional Research Program, University of California, 1988.

Beckham, B. *The Black Student's Guide to College.* New York: Dutton, 1981.

Boyer, E. L. *Campus Life: In Search of Community.* Princeton, N.J.: Carnegie Foundation for the Advancement of Teaching, 1990.

Buffington, P. W. "Hints of Suspicion." *Sky,* March 1990, p. 102.

Dubin, M. "Anti-Semitic Incidents Rose to Decade High." *Tallahassee Democrat,* February 3, 1990, p. 3.

Fauntroy, W. Black History Month keynote speech at Northern Illinois University, DeKalb, Illinois, February 13, 1988.

Gelman, D. "A Much Riskier Passage." *Newsweek,* Summer/Fall 1990 (Special Edition), pp. 10–16.

Goleman, D. "As Bias Crime Seems to Rise, Scientists Study Roots of Racism." *New York Times,* May 29, 1990, pp. B8, B10.

Hively, R. (ed.). *The Lurking Evil: Racial and Ethnic Conflict on the College Campus.* Washington, D.C.: American Association of State Colleges and Universities, 1990.

Ikenberry, S. "Our Students Know Less Than They Should of the Struggle for Civil Rights in Our Country." *Chronicle of Higher Education,* November 30, 1988, p. B5.

Johnston, L. D., O'Malley, P. M., and Bachman, J. G. *Drug Use Among American College Students and Their Non-College-Age Peers, 1976–1987.* Ann Arbor: Institute for Social Research, University of Michigan, 1988.

Louis, E. T. "Black and Blue on Campus." *Essence,* 1986, 17, 67–69.

Muir, D. E. "White Attitudes Toward Blacks at a Deep South University Campus: 1966-1986." *Sociology and Social Research,* 1989, 73, 84–85.

Newcomb, T. M., and Wilson, E. K. (eds.). *College Peer Groups.* Hawthorne, N.Y.: Aldine, 1966.

O'Brien, E. M. "Student Leadership Key to Preventing Racial Conflict, Experts Say." *Black Issues in Higher Education,* 1990, 7, 12.

Pace, C. R. *The Undergraduates: A Report of Their Activities and Progress in the 1980s.* Los Angeles: Center for the Study of Evaluation, 1990.

Perry, W. *Forms of Intellectual and Ethical Development in College Students.* New York: Holt, Rinehart & Winston, 1968.

Radin, C. A. "In 1990 America, Encouraging Word Is Seldom Heard." *Atlanta Constitution,* July 4, 1990, p. 11.

Shaw, K. A. "A Case Study: The President's Role in Creating a Healthy Racial/Ethnic Climate." In R. Hively (ed.), *The Lurking Evil: Racial and Ethnic Conflict on the College Campus.* Washington, D.C.: American Association of State Colleges and Universities, 1990.

Shenk, D. "Young Hate." *CV: The College Magazine,* 1990, 2 (1), 34–39.

Sherrill, J. M., and Siegel, D. G. (eds.). *Responding to Violence on Campus.* New Directions for Student Services, no. 47. San Francisco: Jossey-Bass, 1989.

Whiteley, J. M., and Loxley, J. C. *Character Development in College Students.* Vol. 2. Schenectady, N.Y.: Character Research Press, 1986.

Jon C. Dalton is vice president for student affairs and associate professor of higher education at Florida State University.

Students overwhelmingly interact with others of their own race,
but such patterns can be changed and racist attitudes can be
defused by facilitating new patterns of social interaction.

How White Students and Students of Color Organize and Interact on Campus

Donna M. Bourassa

As Dalton has examined in Chapter One, the current climate on predominantly white college campuses across the United States continues to include subtle and overt forms of racism. This chapter describes the ways in which students of color and white students organize and interact on these campuses. The first section provides a brief profile of today's college students in terms of their readiness to be a part of a multicultural community. The second section examines patterns of interaction among members of different racial groups. The third section describes some sample programs that have been implemented on college campuses to promote positive interactions across racial groups, and considerations for the future conclude the chapter.

Profile of Today's Students

Attitudes, Beliefs, and Behaviors Among White Students. Most research in interracial and interethnic attitudes and perceptions has involved African American and white students (White and Sedlacek, 1987). Clearly, there is a need for more research that examines white student attitudes toward Hispanics, American Indians, and Asians. It is difficult to ascertain whether attitudes held by white students can be generalized to all other racial groups or whether they are specific to a particular racial group.

The following paragraphs describe some of the attitudes, beliefs, and behaviors commonly found among white students with regard to racial interactions.

Uncertainty and Confusion. Many white students are often unsure of how to interpret or respond to the attitudes and behaviors of students of color. According to Williams and others (1987), "for the most part, white students are often mystified by black sensitivity and anger. 'I feel like I can't say anything,' complains UCLA sophomore Tim Pico. 'If you try to help them, they don't like it. No matter what I say, somebody will twist it to where I'm a racist or just a bleeding-heart liberal'" (p. 13).

Fear and Discomfort. Numerous articles (Barol and others, 1983; Turner, 1985; Louis, 1986) have drawn attention to the feelings of awkwardness and fear experienced by white students who have never socially interacted with people from other racial or ethnic groups. Students tend to feel safer with people from their own racial group. Hence, white students and students of color often voluntarily separate themselves. Students clustering by racial group in dining halls, for example, is one of many visible signs of racial tension on campuses.

Misunderstanding, Denial, and Resentment. Many expressions of outward hostility by white students are rooted in ignorance and lack of awareness of racial cultures other than their own. In examining racial incidents, Turner (1985) states that "while whites view the calling of derogatory names or the playing out of cruel jokes as folly, black students said [sic] the incidents are no less painful or troubling" (p. 20).

Many white students deny that racism still exists; they feel that everything is unnecessarily considered a "race issue." Furthermore, some are speaking out about what they believe is "reverse discrimination." Louis (1986) reports that it is easy for many white students to believe that affirmative action is a "free ride" for African American students. As noted in Chapter One, these beliefs have stirred a white backlash evidenced by the emergence of white student unions, protests against the continuation of support programs for students of color, and rallies calling for equal employment of whites.

Sensitivity and the Role of the White Ally. Some white students are taking the issue of racism to heart and are asking themselves what they can do to make a difference. These students are examining their own racist attitudes and behaviors, seeking strategies for self-change, and looking for ways to get their white peers engaged in similar processes.

White students who take on the role of ally often encounter frustration and may become disillusioned when their white peers remain disinterested. In addition, some experience alienation from their white peers who ask them, "Whose side are you on?" Some white students experience disappointment when students of color are not openly appreciative of their efforts. They need to learn not to expect praise from students of color for doing what is right.

These attitudes, beliefs, and behaviors represent some of the major themes described in the literature. The broad spectrum of white student responses to their social responsibility for racism and to the need for meaningful racial interactions ranges from insensitivity and lack of awareness to deep-seated commitment to racial harmony and equality. Turner (1985) reports the observations of this range of response that Rhett Jones, a Brown University professor, noted: "In the past two years Brown has been a veritable hotbed of student activism, and he has seen an increase in cross-racial friendships between students . . . along with active biracial support for such issues as the abolition of apartheid and nuclear disarmament. At the same time, however, he said he has seen more white conservative students who have expressed indifference to or subtle disdain for Afro-Americans and other minorities" (p. 20).

In Chapter Five, Mann and Moser examine in more detail some of the reasons for such diverse attitudes and beliefs, as suggested by theories of racial identity development.

Social Pressures Faced by Students of Color. The social atmosphere encountered by students of color is often unresponsive to their developmental needs. Most students of color on predominantly white campuses experience higher dropout rates and greater social alienation than their white counterparts (Astin, 1982; Suen, 1983; Loo and Rollison, 1986). In examining the social adjustment needs of African Americans and other minorities, Fleming (1981) states, "Although most of our evidence comes from studies of black students, our daily experiences suggest that the same problems are encountered by other minorities as well" (p. 279). Some of the challenges most commonly faced by students of color regarding racial interactions are described in the following paragraphs.

Alienation, Anger, and Frustration. Research findings indicate "the sociocultural alienation of minority students in a predominantly white university is greater than that of white students and that feelings of cultural domination and ethnic isolation are the forms in which the alienation is experienced" (Loo and Rollison, 1986, p. 71). For example, on campuses with small numbers of students of color, it is difficult for them to find and interact with each other. In assessing the quality of campus life, many students of color find that policies and activities are designed for white students, and they find that the same thing holds true in the academic environment. These practices result in feelings of anger, frustration, and helplessness among students of color.

Hsia (1987–88) draws attention to another form of alienation experienced by Asian Americans. The author states that the greater-than-average selectivity used in admitting Asian Americans has resulted in students who are likely to perform at higher academic levels. "This can only build resentment among ethnic groups . . . and could alienate Asian Americans from each other and from their majority and minority classmates" (p. 97).

Mistrust and Uncertainty. For some students of color, college is the first time they have lived or learned in an integrated environment. Many arrive with a set of historical experiences that lead to mistrust and uncertainty about whites (Pounds, 1987). Therefore, one of the challenges these students face is learning to trust white peers, faculty, and student affairs staff.

Pressure to Assimilate. Students of color are often expected to absorb, accept, and adapt to the dominant white culture. For example, Quevedo-Garcia (1987) states that assimilation can be an option taken by Hispanic students who view relationships with the dominant culture as positive and place no value on maintaining their own cultural identity.

Mobilization to Reclaim a Sense of Power. Among student affairs professionals, debate about whether or not student activism is present today on college campuses is commonplace. In particular, student affairs staff seem to be questioning whether activism among students of color like that demonstrated during the civil rights movement is reemerging.

Unfortunately, there is still a need for students of color to hold institutions accountable for responding to their groups' needs and for taking a proactive stance against incidents of racism. Therefore, we see evidence of students of color mobilizing to ensure that these issues are addressed (Pounds, 1987).

Nature of Interracial Contact

In reflecting on the attitudes, beliefs, and behaviors of white students as well as the social pressures faced by students of color, we can safely characterize the general state of the relationships between white students and students of color as tentative at best—tension and absence of closeness are common. Examples of voluntary separatism, such as the lack of interracial partying or the social segregation within the fraternity and sorority systems, are still plentiful on most campuses.

Research in the areas of interracial contact and interracial acceptance of African American, white, and Hispanic adolescents indicates that these three racial groups prefer same-race friends (Clark, 1986). In addition, when cross-race friendships occur in majority white settings, they are generally initiated by students of color and rarely reciprocated by their white peers. Offers of friendship by white students or students of color are often misunderstood. While the offers may be well intended, students of all racial groups tend to suspect the person reaching out of such motives as tokenism or the desire for a "liberal" image. Finally, one-on-one relationships are more common than group encounters for members of different racial groups.

Carter and Sedlacek (1984) cited research by Amir in 1969 on conditions that are unfavorable for interracial contact: "According to Amir, unfavorable conditions . . . are situations in which (a) the groups are in competition with one another (e.g., student organizations competing for funds); (b) involuntary, tense, and unpleasant situations (e.g., arbitrary assignments of roommates from different groups); (c) when one group is perceived as having lower status in the situation (e.g., students think blacks with less ability are admitted); (d) when members of the group are in a state of frustration (i.e., recent defeats or failures, economic difficulties); (e) for minority or majority groups, when minority is of lower status (pp. 11-12).

Carter and Sedlacek (1984) also summarize Amir's report on favorable conditions that reduce racial tensions:

> Favorable conditions are (a) where both groups have contact with one another and members have equal status . . . ; (b) when minority group members have higher status than the majority group members in contact situations . . . ; (c) when an "authority figure" or the social climate are in favor of and promote intergroup contact . . . ; (d) when contact is intimate rather than casual (i.e., frequency, proximity, and nature of contact); (e) when the intergroup contact is rewarding and gratifying; (f) when the members of both groups interact to promote important activities, or to develop some common goals, or goals which meet the objective of both groups and are higher ranking in importance than the individual goals of either group [p. 12].

Obviously, student affairs administrators should work to ensure that favorable conditions are present whenever they are providing programs and services for the campus community.

Programs That Promote Positive Racial Interaction

Student affairs professionals need to develop and support multiple interventions that take into account the distinct needs of white students and students of color. To date, most of the programming interventions described in the literature are those initiated by student affairs practitioners. Many of these interventions seem to lack direct student involvement during the planning or implementation stage. While administrative and institutional responses are necessary for creating change in the campus environment, students also need to be more involved if a campus community is to achieve its highest potential.

Students may become involved in a variety of ways. For example, decision-making committees responsible for new initiatives or policy matters might include racially diverse student representation. Another example would be to encourage and support students in initiating their own programming interventions. In essence, student affairs practitioners need to listen and respond to student voices. Thus, many of the programs to promote positive race relations described here are those that have successfully involved students or were initiated by students. A comprehensive effort should include program interventions aimed at all three distinct audiences: white students only, students of color only, and all of them together.

Programs That Challenge White Students. A study designed to measure attitudes of whites toward African Americans and Hispanics in social situations found that white students held more negative attitudes toward African Americans and Hispanics when race was noted than when it was not. White students were administered a version of the Situational Attitude Scale (SAS). The forms were identical except for the insertion of racial background in one of the forms. For example, Situation A on Form A read "You meet your new roommate," and on Form B this situation read "You meet your new Hispanic roommate." The authors concluded that "successful campus programming to achieve a positive multicultural environment requires work with white students, faculty, and staff, not just more programming involving minority persons" (White and Sedlacek, 1987, p. 180).

Similarly, Katz (1978) observed that in order for changes to occur in response to racism, whites must become involved in understanding their own whiteness. Katz developed a model that sequences the six stages necessary for reeducating whites. The stages focus on the following themes: Stage One—Racism: Definitions and Inconsistencies; Stage Two—Confronting the Reality of Racism; Stage Three—Dealing with Feelings; Stage Four—Cultural Differences: Exploring Cultural Racism; Stage Five—The Meaning of Whiteness: Individual Racism; and Stage Six—Developing Action Strategies. Katz (1978) also describes specific exercises, workshop designs, and guidelines for facilitators of these reeducation programs.

Many colleges and universities have adapted Katz's six-stage model in designing program interventions. For example, Indiana University designed a comprehensive "Training for Trainers" program based on this model. This program prepared faculty, staff, and administrators to provide educational programs and workshops for a variety of campus groups. The program was repeated several times to create an ongoing pool of qualified trainers representative of the community. One of the strengths of the program was its sustained momentum in systematically addressing issues of racism over time. The high level of interest and participation created a ripple effect; particularly among whites in the campus community at large. Another strength was that the responsibility for addressing racism was shared among all the trainers; collaborative partnerships formed among faculty, staff, and administrators (Lorenz and Shipton, 1986). A second example is found at Pennsylvania State University where workshops based on Katz's model yielded attitude changes in approximately 85 percent of the 1,100 participants (Jones, 1987).

A similar programming approach, a support group called "White Allies Against Racism," was developed at the University of Massachusetts, Amherst. Over the last several years, the Office of Human Relations has offered white students, faculty, and staff the opportunity to participate in a six- to eight-week seminar. In the course of this seminar, whites examine their own attitudes and beliefs, acknowledge their own distancing behaviors, identify barriers to change, and develop strategies for facilitating change. Participants are expected to develop specific action plans outlining their "next steps" and to contract with another member for ongoing follow-up on their progress.

In summary, programming interventions for white students should result in heightened levels of awareness about the dynamics of racism. White students should be challenged by these interventions to create attitudinal and behavioral changes that result in an atmosphere that promotes positive race relations. In contrast, programming interventions for students of color are intended to support and empower these students, helping them to achieve in spite of the effects of racism. However, my intent here is not to suggest that challenge and support are mutually exclusive; ideally, all programs should provide degrees of both. Yet the emphasis should vary depending on the population that programmers are trying to impact.

Programs That Support Students of Color. Many of the programming interventions aimed at meeting the needs of students of color focus on orientation activities, peer counseling, support groups, minority student organizations, cultural centers and events, and heritage activities. These types of programs, while they are the most commonly cited, in no way represent an exhaustive list. Also, while there are some commonalities among students of color, important differences exist among major racial identity groups (Livingston and Stewart, 1987). Student affairs professionals need to be aware of these differences and ensure that the specific needs of Asian Americans, African Americans, Hispanics, Native Americans, and the subgroups within each of these groups are met.

Boyer (1987) states, "The spirit of community will be sustained by a climate on the campus where personal relationships are prized, where integrity is the hallmark of discourse, and where people speak and listen to each other carefully" (p. 57). Boyer goes on to state that campuses must place greater emphasis on providing meaningful orientation programs for all students if we are to achieve a spirit of community. To this end, two programming objectives for students of color during this orientation period are (1) practical skill development related to academic preparedness and (2) the identification of role models and support persons (Livingston and Stewart, 1987). In addition, first-week activities should promote interaction between students of color and white students.

At the University of Florida, the "Wake Up Everybody" orientation program was initiated to create an inviting atmosphere for students of color (Parker, Scott, and Chambers, 1985). Students have the opportunity to interact socially with the faculty, and many faculty members serve as special friends throughout the orientation period. The campus compliments these orientation efforts by sponsoring such programs as monthly study breaks involving student affairs staff and students of color; an ethnic walk-in service staffed by counselors who are African American, Hispanic, and Asian; and ongoing efforts to recruit multiethnic students, faculty, and staff.

Many campuses provide various types of peer counseling programs for students of color. Howard (1986) overviews the benefits and requirements of establishing effective peer counseling programs. Howard's support for these programs stems from recognizing the high degree of influence that peers have on each other as role models and providers of support. For example, Radford University instituted a peer program, Casa Amaya, to meet the needs of Chicano students in the residence halls (Crouse, 1985). The counseling center staff assisted students with creating a peer network that could function as a substitute family in response to the importance of family and extended family structures in Chicano culture.

Common to many campuses is the existence of minority student orga-nizations and cultural centers. Rooney (1985) documents the value of these structures; they often offer the primary way for students of color to meet their needs of affiliation, support, and involvement. However, the existence of and support for such programs are often debated. Debate over the establishment of a minority cultural center at Ohio State University, for example, resulted in these viewpoints (Livingston and Stewart, 1987): "Sup-porters believe that a facility of this nature would be better able to address the needs of minority students . . . by providing a place that students can consider their own. Opponents believe that such a facility is antithetical to the purposes of the university and that a cultural facility, in spite of its merits, would serve to restrict interactions between minority and white students" (p. 45).

Astin (1982) wrote that colleges and universities should provide resources to establish cultural centers so that students of color can foster cultural identity, pride, and the necessary strength to challenge and enrich the traditional values of the institution. It is important to remember that although not all students of color experience the need for such programs, some benefit tremendously from them (Rooney, 1985).

Programs to Promote Positive Interracial Relations. Thus far, the programs described have been primarily intended for white students or for students of color. These categories are somewhat artificial because ultimately all programs impact the whole campus community. In addition to these efforts, campuses need to provide social opportunities specifically aimed at facilitating interactions between white students and students of color. Pro-grams need to be designed that will help students develop familiarity, comfortability, and appreciation for peers from ethnic and racial groups other than their own.

One type of programming intervention that has been implemented at various institutions involves residence-based theme communities that often combine specific experiential living objectives with an academic compo-nent. At the University of Massachusetts, Amherst, students in a residence hall developed a multicultural, multiethnic community during the 1988–89 academic year in an attempt to create an academically and socially supportive environment for students of color. The program has now been expanded to create a place for white students to learn about issues of race and racism. Thus, the program now consists of two parts, "Nuance: Shades of Difference" for students of color and "Aware: Allies Working Against Racism Everywhere" for white students.

In practice, the students of color in Nuance develop their own educational and social programs. Some of the programs are designed for students of color only while others are for the entire residence hall community. White students involved with Aware can elect to take a one-credit course to learn about the dynamics of racism. The two parts of the program are intended to work both together and independently to offer a broad range of experiences that instill racial harmony. Already students and staff have noticed a marked improvement in racial attitudes and in the degree of student interest in the program.

A second major type of programming intervention found in the literature is the creation of a student group to work together on issues of racism. These programs are designed to promote racial interaction and are intended to join white students and students of color in coalition. Louis (1986) refers to an organization called Students Against Racial Tension (START), formed at Northeastern University to develop ways to improve contact between African Americans and whites. Ponterotto, Grieger, and Heaphy (1985) provide a comprehensive description and evaluation of a group called Students Against Racial Separation (STARS), developed at the University of Virginia. This organization was initiated by a racially mixed group of first-year residence hall students concerned about the degree of racial separatism they experienced. Eventually, students enlisted the help of two consultants from the counseling center. The authors stated that the program's uniqueness and success stemmed from the involvement of students at the grassroots level. The model and recommendations outlined in this article can serve as an excellent reference for campuses interested in establishing a similar group.

Considerations for the Future

A successful college education must prepare all students to live in and contribute to a society that is increasingly racially diverse. Student affairs professionals need to develop a broad range of programming interventions that help students feel ready to interact and benefit from members of all racial groups.

To date, there are a surprisingly limited number of educational strategies addressing racism reported in the student affairs literature. Furthermore, many of these strategies are becoming a bit timeworn. One of the greatest challenges that student affairs practitioners face is ensuring that the scope of interventions goes beyond African American and white relations. We need to become more informed about the relationships between white students and Asian American, American Indian, and Hispanic students. And we have yet to assess the level and type of interactions that exist among racially oppressed groups themselves in order to determine what further support is needed.

Finally, we need to evaluate systematically the usefulness of our current practices. Thus far, the amount of evaluative data on programs designed to foster positive racial interactions and to combat racism is minimal. Such data are desperately needed to allow us to determine whether or not our efforts are achieving our intended outcomes.

References

Astin, A. W. *Minorities in American Higher Education: Recent Trends, Current Prospects, and Recommendations.* San Francisco: Jossey-Bass, 1982.

Barol, B., Camper, D., Pigott, C., Nadolsky, R., and Sarris, M. "Separate Tables: Why White and Black Students Choose to Segregate." *Newsweek on Campus,* March 1983, pp. 4-11.

Boyer, E. L. *College: The Undergraduate Experience in America.* San Francisco: Harper & Row, 1988.

Carter, R. T., and Sedlacek, W. E. *Interracial Contact, Background, and Attitudes: Implications for Campus Programs.* Counseling Center Research Report, no. 13. College Park: University of Maryland, 1984.

Clark, M. L. *The Status of Interethnic Contact and Ethnocentrism Among White, Hispanic, and Black Students.* Paper presented at the annual meeting of the American Educational Research Association, San Francisco, California, April 1986.

Crouse, R. "Using Peer Network Therapy with a Residence Program for Chicano Students." *Journal of College Student Personnel,* 1985, 26, 549-550.

Fleming, J. "Special Needs of Blacks and Other Minorities." In A. W. Chickering and Associates, *The Modern American College: Responding to the New Realities of Diverse Students and a Changing Society.* San Francisco: Jossey-Bass, 1981.

Howard, M. F. "Developing an Effective Peer Counseling Program for Entering Students Who Are Low Income and/or Minority Students." In C. A. Taylor (ed.), *Handbook of Minority Student Services.* Madison, Wisc.: NMCC, 1986.

Hsia, J. "Asian Americans Fight the Myth of the Super Student." *Educational Record,* 1987-88, 68 (4)-69 (1), 94-97.

Jones, W. T. "Enhancing Minority-White Peer Interactions." In D. J. Wright (ed.), *Responding to the Needs of Today's Minority Students.* New Directions for Student Services, no. 38. San Francisco: Jossey-Bass, 1987.

Katz, J. H. *White Awareness: A Handbook for Anti-Racism Training.* Norman: University of Oklahoma Press, 1978.

Livingston, M. D., and Stewart, M. A. "Minority Students on a White Campus: Perceptions in Truth." *NASPA Journal,* 1987, 24 (3), 39-49.

Loo, C. M., and Rollison, G. "Alienation of Ethnic Minority Students at a Predominantly White University." *Journal of Higher Education,* 1986, 57, 58-77.

Lorenz, N., and Shipton, W. *Anti-Racism Training for Trainers Workshop: A Report to the Bloomington Campus.* Bloomington: Indiana University, 1986.

Louis, E. T. "Black and Blue on Campus." *Essence,* 1986, *17,* 67–69.

Parker, W. M., Scott, J., and Chambers, A. "Creating an Inviting Atmosphere for College Students from Ethnic Minority Groups." *Journal of College Student Personnel,* 1985, *26,* 82–87.

Ponterotto, J. G., Grieger, I., and Heaphy, T. J. "Students Together Against Racial Separatism." *Journal of College Student Personnel,* 1985, *26,* 251–253.

Pounds, A. W. "Black Student Needs on Predominantly White Campuses." In D. J. Wright (ed.), *Responding to the Needs of Today's Minority Students.* New Directions for Student Services, no. 38. San Francisco: Jossey-Bass, 1987.

Quevedo-Garcia, E. L. "Facilitating the Development of Hispanic Students." In D. J. Wright (ed.), *Responding to the Needs of Today's Minority Students.* New Directions for Student Services, no. 38. San Francisco: Jossey-Bass, 1987.

Rooney, G. D. "Minority Students' Involvement in Minority Student Organizations: An Exploratory Study." *Journal of College Student Personnel,* 1985, *26* (5), 450–455.

Suen, H. K. "Alienation and Attrition of Black College Students on a Predominantly White Campus." *Journal of College Student Personnel,* 1983, *26,* 117–121.

Turner, R. D. "The Resurgence of Racism on White Campuses." *Black Collegian,* 1985, *4* (2), 18–24.

White, T. J., and Sedlacek, W. E. "White Student Attitudes Toward Blacks and Hispanics: Programming Implications." *Journal of Multicultural Counseling and Development,* 1987, *15,* 171–181.

Williams, D., Crawford, J., Yonce, J., Nomani, A., Allen, T., and Brooks, H. "Is the Dream Over?" *Newsweek on Campus,* February 1987, pp. 10–14.

Donna M. Bourassa is staff development coordinator of Residential Education/ Housing Services at the University of Massachusetts, Amherst.

Precollege characteristics and college experiences affect student
performance and satisfaction, as reported in this study of African
American and white students on a predominantly white campus.

Racial Differences in Student Experiences and Attitudes

Shanette M. Harris, Michael T. Nettles

Some of the challenges faced by students of color and the attitudes, beliefs, and behaviors of white students that promote voluntary group separation were discussed in Chapter Two. To help us understand the dynamics underlying the absence of interracial relationships, this chapter investigates interactions between student background characteristics and college entrance criteria and the behaviors and experiences that students have in college.

Theoretical Model

Theoretical models indicate that several experiences combine to determine students' satisfaction and performance (Bean, 1982; Tinto, 1975). Differences in students' experiences may contribute to conflict and misunderstanding and be a major factor in the increase in conflict that recently has been reported between African American and white students on predominantly white campuses.

The data presented in this chapter are used to test a theoretical model that is based on assumptions outlined by Tinto (1975), Lacy (1978), and Shavelson and Bolus (1982). This model proposes that the behaviors and experiences that students have in college are related to their background characteristics and college entrance criteria. In addition to these variables, student performance and satisfaction are also examined. Three specific questions are addressed: (1) Are there differences in the background characteristics, college experiences, performance, and satisfaction of African American and white students? (2) Are background characteristics and college experiences associated with student performance and satisfaction, and if so, are they associated in the same way for African American and white students? (3) Are the predictors of performance and satisfaction the same for African American and white students? The results of this research are discussed within the context of student social interactions and peer relationships.

Methodology

This study analyzed the responses of African American and white students from the University of Tennessee to two survey instruments, administered in 1987 and 1988: the Student Satisfaction Questionnaire and the Student Experiences Questionnaire (Center for Assessment and Research, 1987). Both questionnaires were designed to obtain specific information about students' college experiences. The Student Satisfaction Questionnaire was developed to measure the experiences of students currently enrolled at the university. The Student Experiences Questionnaire, subtitled "A Look Back," was developed to assess the experiences of students who had attended the university but had withdrawn before degree completion (dropouts). The instruments assess students' reactions to general services, experiences with their major program, classroom experiences, social interactions, academic experiences, and overall satisfaction with the university.

Five background characteristics were included in this research (gender, race, high school grade point average, ACT scores, and age), and data for all five variables were obtained from student records. Data for the college experiences, satisfaction, and performance variables were obtained from the two student surveys and from student records. Three variables were used to assess college experiences in this study: level of campus involvement, amount of faculty-student interaction, and satisfaction with courses. The level of campus involvement reflects students' participation in the campus environment outside of the classroom. The amount of faculty-student interaction refers to the number of faculty members that students know well enough to ask for a letter of reference or recommendation, and satisfaction with courses refers to the degree to which students enjoyed the information imparted in class. Performance was represented by students' cumulative grade point average (GPA) and persistence toward degree completion. Finally, satisfaction refers to students' reported level of overall satisfaction with the university.

Results

Table 3.1 shows the number and percentage of African American and white students participating in the study according to gender. Table 3.2 provides similar information for students by race and persistence (those who remained at the university versus those who left the university before degree completion). Table 3.3 shows the means and F scores for each variable of interest for African American and white students. Table 3.4 shows the same information for each variable for males and females. Table 3.5 presents the means and F scores for each variable of the race and gender interaction. Tables 3.6 and 3.7 present the results related to persistence. Specifically, Table 3.6 summarizes the means and F scores for persisters and students who left early, and Table 3.7 shows the means and F scores for race and the two levels of persistence. Chi-square analyses and univariate analyses of variance were used to analyze the data.

Table 3.1. Weighted Chi-Square Test Comparing African American and White Students by Gender

Variable	African American		White		Chi-Square
Gender	%	n	%	n	0.0147
Male	41	96	49	2152	
Female	59	138	51	2201	

Table 3.2. Weighted Chi-Square Test Comparing African American and White Students by Persistence

Variable	African American		White		Chi-Square
Persistence	%	n	%	n	0.0001
Dropout	66	156	53	2333	
Remain	33	78	47	2028	

Table 3.3. Summary of Means Comparing White and African American Students

Variable	White Mean	African American Mean	F
Cumulative College GPA	2.45	2.08	16.66[a]
High School GPA	3.15	3.10	1.449
ACT Score	21.41	18.08	29.56[a]
Age	21.63	21.27	0.6357
Satisfaction	−0.0062	−0.2258	2.566
Campus Involvement	0.1408	0.4537	9.470[b]
Faculty Involvement	−0.0119	−0.0709	0.0019
Courses	−0.0208	−0.2011	2.432

[a] Significant at 0.01 level.

[b] Significant at 0.001 level.

Table 3.4. Summary of Means Comparing Males and Females

Variable	Female Mean	Male Mean	F
Cumulative College GPA	2.44	2.42	1.588
High School GPA	3.17	3.04	0.0136
ACT Score	20.23	22.26	21.43[a]
Age	21.28	21.85	10.51[a]
Satisfaction	0.0206	0.0548	0.4564
Campus Involvement	0.1615	0.1509	0.1161
Faculty Involvement	-0.0055	-0.0241	2.388
Courses	-0.0238	-0.0833	0.0215

[a] Significant at 0.001 level.

Table 3.5. Summary of Means for Race and Gender Interaction

Variable	African American Males	White Males	African American Females	White Females	F
Cumulative College GPA	2.246	2.427	1.991	2.476	3.452[a]
High School GPA	3.250	3.039	3.101	3.175	6.263
ACT Score	20.03	22.33	17.09	20.45	1.020
Age	21.96	21.84	20.93	21.41	1.738
Satisfaction	-0.595	-0.546	-0.3090	0.0438	2.427
Campus Involvement	0.5093	0.1389	0.4284	0.1427	0.1419
Faculty Involvement	0.1864	-0.0313	-0.1996	0.0081	3.601
Courses	-0.1402	-0.0814	-0.2315	0.0418	0.9781

[a] Significant at < 0.06 level.

Table 3.6. Summary of Means for Persistence

Variable	Dropout Mean	Persistors Mean	F
Cumulative College GPA	2.118	2.2780	120.03[a]
High School GPA	3.008	3.220	26.60[a]
ACT Score	20.32	22.27	15.61[a]
Age	21.16	22.11	26.15[a]
Satisfaction	-0.3352	0.3326	38.36[a]
Campus Involvement	0.2106	0.0957	0.5879
Faculty Involvement	-0.3608	0.3634	37.98[a]
Courses	-0.1954	0.1524	3.508

[a] Significant at 0.001 level.

Table 3.7. Summary of Means for Race and Persistence Interaction

Variable	African American		White		F
	Left	Remained	Left	Remained	
Cumulative College GPA	1.705	2.589	2.141	2.789	2.854[a]
High School GPA	3.005	3.353	3.008	3.214	1.747
ACT Score	17.22	19.25	20.50	22.41	0.0154
Age	20.75	22.00	21.19	22.11	0.5461
Satisfaction	-0.4687	0.1104	-0.3275	0.3426	2.2031
Campus Involvement	0.4705	0.4305	0.1956	0.0806	0.1377
Faculty Involvement	-0.2797	0.2181	0.3655	0.3699	1.410
Courses	-0.2097	-0.1891	-0.1946	0.1678	2.795[a]

[a] Significant at < 0.09 level.

These data suggest the following statistically significant conclusions:

1. Fewer African American males were enrolled, and they had higher high school grade point averages than the other groups.
2. Males received higher scores on the ACT.
3. Male students were older than females.
4. African Americans scored lower on the ACT than white students.
5. A greater percentage of African American students left the university than white students.
6. African American students received lower college grades than white students.
7. African American students, as compared to white students, had greater campus involvement.
8. African American males and white females had the highest level of faculty involvement, and African American females had the lowest level.
9. African American students were less satisfied with the university than white students.
10. Persisters had higher high school grades, higher ACT scores, higher cumulative grade point averages, greater involvement with faculty, were older, viewed courses more positively, were more satisfied with the university, and were more likely to be white than those who left the university before degree completion.

Discussion

A major question addressed by this study is whether or not students had similar college experiences and background characteristics. Within the limitations of the sample studied, it appears that the answer to this question depends on race and gender. Race effects were indicated by the findings that African Americans earned lower scores on the ACT, received lower college grades, had greater campus involvement, were less satisfied with their courses and the total university, and left the university before completing their degree more often than did their white counterparts.

Some of the findings also depended on the gender of the respondents. Consistent with previous research findings, males received higher scores on the ACT than females. The male students tended to be older than females. Although African American males were not well represented in the sample, they did have higher high school grades than any other group. African American males and white females also had the highest level of involvement with faculty, while African American females had the lowest level of faculty involvement and the lowest college grades.

The differences between African American and white students were generally similar across genders, but some exceptions existed. In terms of faculty contact and college grades, African American females encountered greater difficulties than African American males. African American males and white females had the highest level of faculty involvement, while African American females had the lowest. Previous research has suggested that contact with faculty influences student attitudes and behaviors toward academic performance and persistence in colleges and universities (Pascarella, 1984; Tinto, 1975). Nettles and Johnson (1987) reported that students who had frequent interactions with faculty were better socialized than those who did not. Our study supports these findings and also suggests that the effects of both race and gender are important in understanding students' perceptions of interactions with faculty members.

The finding that African American females had the lowest level of involvement with faculty is consistent with studies that have suggested that African American females seem more positively affected by attending predominantly African American institutions (Pascarella, Smart, and Stoecker, 1989) than by attending predominantly white institutions. The implication that attending a predominantly white university has negative effects for African American females was further supported by the finding that they received lower college grades than either white females, African American males, or white males. In contrast to African American females, African American males appear to receive some beneficial effects by interacting with faculty. The finding that white females received higher grades than other groups supports the view that the university system and schools in general are more accepting of certain standards of behavior, which include politeness, a nonthreatening style of presentation, and passivity. In comparison to other groups, white females are more likely to conform to these behavioral standards.

One partial explanation for the differences between African American males and females on grades and faculty involvement is that African American males may enter the university at different stages of racial identity than African American females. Parham and Helms (1985) found that African American male students were more likely to adhere to attitudes of the preencounter stage (that is, the stage when an individual thinks of the world as the opposite of African American). In contrast, African American females were more likely to adhere to attitudes of the internalization stage of identity (when concentration on other factors is as important as focusing on one's racial group). Similarly, Hughes (1987) conducted a phenomenological study and found that African American females, in comparison to African American males, "express greater inner strength, a view of self as capable and confident and having the capacity to withstand negative external stimuli" (p. 541). Females with these characteristics may be less inclined to seek assistance with academic problems because they are confident that they can cope with stressors without involving others. In contrast, African American males who enter the university in the preencounter stage of racial identity may have lower self-esteem, which increases the likelihood that they will form close relationships with faculty. They are not as confident as their female counterparts that they can cope with stressors alone. Thus, differences in the values and attitudes of African American males and females when they enter the university may lead to differences in their behavior on campus.

The most obvious findings of our study were the differences between African American and white students on background characteristics and college experiences. Previous findings emphasize similar differences, although explanations of the differences have varied (Beasley and Sease, 1974; Clark and Plotkin, 1964; Gibbs, 1973; Nettles, Thoeny, and Gosman, 1986; Pruitt, 1973; Sedlacek, Brooks, Mindus, 1968; Stanley and Porter, 1967). However, few if any of these studies have considered the significance of background characteristics and college experiences for the development of peer relations between African American and white students. Our study's findings, in conjunction with theories from social psychology, may help reveal how the characteristics that students bring into the university and the experiences they have after enrollment influence their development of different types of personal relationships. Without further empirical research to verify the relationships among these factors, however, it is difficult to specify directly the mechanisms through which peer relations are formed, maintained, and in some instances terminated.

Significantly fewer African American males were present in our sample. This finding reflects the decreasing number of African American males who enroll in four-year institutions in general and specifically who enroll at predominantly white colleges (Marks, 1986). This imbalance in the number of males and females differed sharply from the representation of white males and females, which was in almost a one-to-one ratio. During the college years, students attempt to integrate various facets of themselves, including the academic, vocational, social, and interpersonal. Interactions with peer groups assist in promoting this sense of identity. Unlike white students, African American students on predominantly white campuses have a smaller pool of people like themselves with whom to establish relationships and from whom to receive support as they attempt to resolve concerns specific to the stages of their development.

An unequal representation of males and females on predominantly white campuses has implications for the interpersonal development of both African American and white students, particularly African American females (Fleming, 1984). African American females have fewer opportunities to establish meaningful relationships with their male counterparts. The relationships between the racial groups became even more complex when African American males enter the university with preencounter attitudes that lead them to form intimate relationships with white females (Parham and Helms, 1981). Some of the interracial tension experienced on white campuses has been associated with African American male and white female dating patterns. Inequities in the number of African American males and females may not have negative effects on the developmental needs of African American males, white females, and white males, but they may lead to neglect of the belonging needs of African American females (Styles, 1969). The fact that fewer white male and African American female relationships are formed also emphasizes the isolation that some females can experience.

African American students received lower scores on the ACT than white students. Entering a university at a disadvantage affects students' expectations for future performance by decreasing their sense of self-efficacy. The knowledge that these students do not enter with the same credentials may combine with white students' feelings of resentment about affirmative action and minority student programming and lead white students to feel that minorities are receiving "unfair attention." The theory of fundamental attribution error (Ross, 1977) would predict that white students might attribute African American students' lower ACT scores to a lack of ability and competence as opposed to external factors such as socioeconomic status and deficits in high school training. In addition, if students hold these thoughts prior to meeting African American students, they would tend to adhere more strongly to the negative information, even in the face of learning more positive facts. Whether differences in ACT scores and college grades are self-produced or are influenced by subtle forms of racist behavior, differences are perceived as negative, and they perpetuate separation along racial lines. White students' behaviors are associated with certain beliefs that have an impact on African American students' perceptions of themselves. That is, African American students may begin to perceive themselves as academically inferior after entering the university because they internalize the covert and overt messages of white students and faculty. Some of their thoughts likely originate from parental and community teachings as well. Just as white parents indirectly and directly teach their children that African Americans are less competent, African American parents, in efforts to protect their own, teach similar prejudiced messages. As a result, African American students may enter the university with thoughts that white students do not expect them to be successful. On the other hand, the self-efficacy of white students is positively influenced by their background characteristics. They enter the university with higher ACT scores and continue to receive higher college grades. These differences between African American and white students reinforce white students' preexisting thoughts and feelings of superiority, which were probably promoted by parents and their community. As a result, both groups of students experience discomfort in the presence of the other because they perceive themselves to be different. These perceived differences are magnified by the cultural reality of competition for scarce resources (in this case, high grades) within the college environment.

In many instances, African American students seek camaraderie and support from other segments of the university, as revealed by our finding that African American students had greater campus involvement than white students. Involvement and affiliation with offices and individuals unrelated to the classroom setting serve a useful function in students' growth. However, interactions outside the class may also interfere with establishing relationships with white students. This is supported by research indicating that African American students form bonds with other African American students or community members (Barol and others, 1983; Loo and Rollison, 1986; Webster and Sedlacek, 1982).

African American students may seek greater campus involvement to increase their positive experiences and balance their dislike for university courses. This dissatisfaction with their courses may be related to the presentation and content of the material. Faculty have traditionally prepared and presented courses from a Eurocentric perspective (Bennett, 1988). Such an orientation indirectly promotes division between African American and white students by neglecting the values, contributions, and worldview of the ancestors of students descended from non-European cultures. This tendency is particularly significant for white students who enter the university with negative attitudes toward African American students originating from parental teachings, peer interactions, and an absence of interracial relationships. It is likely that African American students would be perceived more positively by white American students if they were taught to appreciate the culture and contributions of African American students' ancestors. Yet the expectation exists by both white and African American students that African American students should be able to rationalize the importance of the courses in order to perform well and persist through the program. In contrast, white students are able to learn about themselves and their ancestors within the classroom setting. This privilege provides white students with a purpose and sense of meaning that instills racial pride and group cohesion. Thus, the classroom empowers white students to confront other college stressors. On the other hand, African American students struggle with internal conflict and ambivalence as they strive for excellence in the face of external evidence that suggests they are not an integral part of the university.

In the instances when white and African American students attempt to gravitate toward each other, issues of trust and attraction become particularly important. The equity and reward theories of attraction can be used to understand the dynamics of exchanges between African American and white students that have recently resulted in tension and misunderstanding. Equity theory proposes that an individual will be attracted to someone under the condition that what is received from the relationship is proportional to what he or she contributes to it (Walster, Walster, and Berscheid, 1978). But equity is difficult to achieve when white students enter the exchange at a disadvantage resulting from previous prejudicial parental teachings and the failure of school systems to impart a global and multicultural educational experience. African American students live within white culture and have mastered the values, norms, and standard ways of relating. But white students' exposure to peers of color has usually been limited, and in many instances, the information acquired has been distorted. Thus, the African American student who is approached by a white student has to weigh the costs and benefits of the relationship because it is likely that he or she will have to teach the other about African American culture and values. According to equity theory, if the relationship is perceived as inequitable, a participant will first attempt to restore equity by setting things right. However, according to Steele (1988), in order for white students to feel comfortable interfacing with African American students, they must believe that their racial innocence will be confirmed by African American students. Thus, they indirectly agree to take away their guilt. Depending on the African American students' stage of racial identity and value system, they may not attempt to absolve white students of their guilt but rather hope to assist them with exposing and then resolving feelings of guilt. Just as African American students perceive teaching about their culture as inequitable, white students perceive that facing internal feelings and thoughts of prejudice is uncomfortable and thus inequitable. As a result of perceived inequities, one or both participants terminate the relationship before it progresses to more than a superficial level.

The reward theory of attraction proposes that students will like others whose behavior is rewarding to them or who have been associated with rewarding events (Lott and Lott, 1974). It is difficult to define precisely events that are rewarding for all students. However, it is likely that students' peer associations before entering college are good indicators of whether interracial relationships will be established during the college years. If previous interracial relationships have been characterized by positive experiences, students are more likely to establish and maintain similar relationships in college. Based on the upsurge in racial violence on predominantly white college campuses, however, it can be assumed that the majority of African American and white students are unfamiliar with each other and do not socialize on a frequent basis.

In summary, African American and white students enter universities with different background characteristics, which interact with the college environment to produce varied college experiences. The differences between the two groups may account for racial conflict and tension as well as for different levels of progress and academic persistence.

Implications for College Interventions

How do universities approach this multifaceted social problem that is reflected in the interactions of our future leaders? At this time, the answer is unclear because the exact nature of the problem has not been determined.

The first task is to obtain a more thorough understanding of the specific issues involved in combating interracial tension on campus by posing questions and conducting well-designed empirical research. Problem specification and research should be approached from a broad, multilevel perspective. College students do not exhibit behaviors in a vacuum; rather, racial tensions and misunderstandings begin at the early stages of development and build through the years. As a result, effective efforts must include interventions targeted at all levels of education in our society.

Universities can assist in designing interventions aimed at eradicating racial strife by concentrating on students enrolled at elementary and high school levels. Targeting early levels of development is likely to be more effective than attempting to change thoughts and behaviors that students have reinforced over many years. Schools of education within universities can also modify courses for prospective teachers to include a multiculturally diverse curriculum. Often, the beliefs and behaviors of teachers have a significant influence on the future values and behaviors of their students. In addition, education programs must make a concerted effort to recruit people of color who are interested in teaching careers. As more opportunities have become available in disciplines other than education, fewer students are seeking careers as teachers. Yet the minority population continues to grow, and the presence of minority teachers is needed to assist other teachers and to serve as role models for students before the college years.

Focusing on elementary and high school levels of the educational system does not relieve institutions of higher learning of their own responsibilities. College administrators, staff, and faculty have an obligation to provide campus learning conditions that are appropriate for all students in our society.

An interactional approach to changing student and university characteristics suggests several strategies for reducing the amount of racial tension experienced by college students. This approach assumes that change in either system will produce change in the other. Because there are multiple causes for racial difficulties, we will need multiple strategies, including those that involve faculty and administrators, single-race groups, groups with culturally diverse members, formal programs, and informal programs.

Several interventions for instituting change in the college environment have already been designed. They include models for program development, peer-initiated programs, prejudice reduction workshops, and residence-based theme communities. All of these interventions can be employed in an interactional framework to combat current concerns. The most effective approach is likely to combine student programs and services with university modifications.

In addition to attempting to reduce racial tension, programs should be designed and implemented that reduce the impact of prejudice on students, as prejudice is sometimes unavoidable. Variables that mediate the tension can be the focus of campus interventions. For example, programs and services that target the attributions that students make about the behaviors of different groups as well as skills development workshops that teach African American students and other minorities how to handle various situations involving prejudice and racism can provide students with a sense of control and well-being. Through training, interpersonal problem-solving skills can be enhanced that will increase students' ability to find alternative solutions to racial conflict and feelings of anger, frustration, and discomfort.

Other mediating variables can also be the target of intervention efforts. Recruitment efforts geared toward equalizing the number of African American males and females, the promotion of minority participation in university clubs and organizations, the development of course curricula that focus on cultural diversity by referring to the contributions of all groups traditionally referred to as minorities, and the recruitment of minority faculty would make the campus environment more hospitable for minority and majority student interactions. Based on our results, providing role models for African American females might be especially significant to their well-being.

Finally, programs that enhance students' own coping abilities and increase the resources that they can use in dealing with racial problems will empower them in the midst of tension. Removing racial stressors or minimizing their effects is the preferred goal, but many of the problems inherent in bringing diverse populations together are not solvable. The ability to employ personal coping strategies and problem-solving skills to influence the environment thus becomes essential.

References

Barol, B., Camper, D., Pigott, C., Nadolsky, R., and Sarris, M. "Separate Tables: Why White and Black Students Choose to Segregate." *Newsweek on Campus*, March 1983, pp. 4-11.

Bean, J. P. "Dropouts and Turnover: The Synthesis and Test of a Causal Model of Student Attrition." *Research in Higher Education*, 1980, *12*, 155-187.

Beasley, S. R., and Sease, W. A. "Using Biographical Data as a Predictor of Academic Success for Black University Students." *Journal of College Student Personnel*, 1974, *15*, 201-206.

Bennett, W. J. "Why the West?" *National Review*, 1988, *40*, 37-39.

Center for Assessment and Research. "Student Satisfaction Questionnaire" and "Student Experiences Questionnaire: A Look Back." Knoxville, Tenn.: Center for Assessment and Research, 1987.

Clark, K. B., and Plotkin, L. *The Negro Student at Integrated Colleges*. New York: National Scholarship Service and Fund for Negro Students, 1964.

Fleming, J. *Blacks in College: A Comparative Study of Students' Success in Black and in White Institutions*. San Francisco: Jossey-Bass, 1984.

Gibbs, J. L. "Black Students/White University: Different Expectations." *Personnel and Guidance Journal*, 1973, *51*, 463-469.

Hughes, M. S. "Black Students' Participation in Higher Education." *Journal of College Student Personnel*, 1987, *28* (6), 532-545.

Lacy, W. B. "Interpersonal Relationships as Mediators of Structural Effects: College Student Socialization in a Traditional and an Experimental University Environment." *Sociology of Education*, 1978, *58*, 201-211.

Loo, C. M., and Rollison, G. "Alienation of Ethnic Minority Students at a Predominantly White University." *Journal of Higher Education*, 1986, *57*, 58-77.

Lott, A. J., and Lott, B. E. "The Role of Reward in the Formation of Positive Interpersonal Attitudes." In T. Huston (ed.), *Foundations of Interpersonal Attrition*. New York: Academic Press, 1974.

Marks, J. L. *The Enrollment of Black Students in Education: Can Declines Be Prevented?* Atlanta, Ga.: Southern Regional Education Board, 1986.

Nettles, M. T., and Johnson, J. R. "Race, Sex, and Other Factors as Determinants of College Students' Socialization." *Journal of College Student Personnel*, 1987, *28*, 512-524.

Nettles, M. T., Thoeny, A. R., and Gosman, E. J. "Comparative and Predictive Analyses of Black and White Students' College Achievement and Experiences." *Journal of Higher Education*, 1986, *57*, 289-317.

Parham, T. A., and Helms, J. E. "The Influence of Black Students' Racial Identity Attitudes on Preferences for Counselor's Race." *Journal of Counseling Psychology*, 1981, *28*, 250-257.

Parham, T. A., and Helms, J. E. "Relation of Racial Identity Attitudes to Self-Actualization and Affective States of Black Students." *Journal of Counseling Psychology*, 1985, *32*, 431-440.

Pascarella, E. T. "College Environmental Influences on Students' Educational Aspirations." *Journal of Higher Education*, 1984, *55*, 751-771.

Pascarella, E. T., Smart, J. C., and Stoecker, J. "College Race and the Early Status Attainment of Black Students." *Journal of Higher Education*, 1989, *60*, 82-107.

Pruitt, A. S. "Minority Admissions to Large Universities: A Response." *Journal of College Student Personnel*, 1973, *14*, 22-24.

Ross, L. D. "The Intuitive Psychologist and His Shortcomings: Distortions in the Attribution Process." In L. Berkowitz (ed.), *Advances in Experimental Social Psychology*. Vol. 10. New York: Academic Press, 1977.

Sedlacek, W. E., Brooks, G. C., and Mindus, L. "Black and Other Minority Admissions to Large Universities: Three-Year National Trends." *Journal of College Student Personnel*, 1968, *9*, 177-179.

Shavelson, R., and Bolus, R. "Self-Concept: The Interplay of Theory and Methods." *Journal of Educational Psychology*, 1982, *74*, 3-17.

Stanley, J. C., and Porter, A. C. "Correlation of SAT Scores with College Grades for Negroes Versus Whites." *Journal of Educational Measurement*, 1967, *4*, 199-218.

Steele, S. "I'm Black, You're White, Who's Innocent? Race and Power in an Era of Blame." *Harper's Magazine*, June 1988, pp. 45-53.

Styles, M. H. "Personality Characteristics, Self, and Academic Performance of Black Freshmen at a Predominantly White University as Compared with Black Freshmen at a Predominantly Black University." *Dissertation Abstracts International*, 1969, *30*, 5249A.

Tinto, V. "Dropout from Higher Education: A Theoretical Synthesis of Recent Research." *Review of Educational Research*, 1975, *45*, 89-125.

Walster, E., Walster, G. W., and Berscheid, E. *Equity: Theory and Research*. Newton, Mass.: Allyn & Bacon, 1978.

Webster, D. W., and Sedlacek, W. E. "The Differential Impact of a University Student Union on Campus Subgroups." *NASPA Journal*, 1982, *19*, 48-51.

Shanette M. Harris is a licensed clinical psychologist and assistant professor in the Department of Educational and Counseling Psychology, University of Tennessee.

Michael T. Nettles is vice president for assessment for the University of Tennessee.

A peer training model is presented to illustrate how a campus can involve its students, faculty, and administrators in effective prejudice-reducing strategies.

Peer Training Strategies for Welcoming Diversity

Cherie R. Brown, George J. Mazza

The National Coalition-Building Institute (NCBI) is a nonprofit leadership training organization that has led peer training programs to reduce prejudice on ninety college and university campuses in the United States, Canada, England, Northern Ireland, South Africa, Israel, and the Netherlands (Smith, 1989). This chapter presents the operational assumptions governing NCBI's peer training programs, the theory and methodology of its prejudice reduction model, and a process for developing campus peer training teams, along with a sampling of colleges and universities that have implemented this approach.

Operational Assumptions

Training Teams of Peer Leaders Is the Most Effective Way to Empower People to Take Leadership in Reducing Racism. College students, faculty, and staff often experience powerlessness in the face of increasing intergroup tensions on campus. For many, the issues are so overwhelming that they do not know how to begin to address them. Often the greatest obstacle to taking action against racism and other forms of discrimination is the sense that individual initiatives have little effect in light of the enormity of the problem. One strategy for overcoming this key obstacle is to train a corps of students, faculty, and staff who then reclaim their own power by leading concrete, replicable prejudice reduction workshops in a variety of college settings. When these individuals are coached to think of themselves as campus prejudice reduction leaders, they become catalysts for deeper institutional changes.

NEW DIRECTIONS FOR STUDENT SERVICES, no. 56, Winter 1991 © Jossey-Bass Inc., Publishers

Prejudice reduction workshops can also be a teaching method for training campus leaders. We have observed that when participants attend a campus training session knowing that they are going to lead prejudice reduction workshops later, their own learning is both more rapid and more profound. The planning and conducting of the workshops reinforce their learning. The effective leading of these workshops requires each peer leader to examine and work through his or her own prejudices. It has often been observed that one learns best by teaching. The peer group leadership of prejudice reduction workshops operates on a similar principle: One learns best by leading.

Programs to Welcome Diversity Require an Ongoing Campuswide Effort. Too often the only systemwide effort to address diversity issues on campus is a two-hour program for students during orientation at the beginning of the autumn term. More needs to be done. Utilizing an in-house training team to conduct ongoing prejudice reduction programs allows colleges to respond more effectively to the issues of discrimination that are present on college campuses. First, the training team is a readily available resource that can be called on throughout the academic year. Second, the training team can respond to the unique needs of a number of different constituencies, such as students in dormitories, private societies, campus clubs, faculty, and service staff. Third, the training team, by including members of diverse backgrounds, is able to respond to concerns that involve particular campus groups as well as to concerns that involve the entire campus (for example, to issues between African Americans and Jews as well as to those between students and faculty). The most effective campus teams include not only students but also faculty, administrators, support staff, and campus police. A campuswide effort to address diversity issues must be mindful of recruiting peer training teams that can work with nonstudent groups. In our experience, training groups composed exclusively of students do not have the same level of ongoing institutional impact as teams composed of students, faculty, and administrators.

The Establishment of Proactive Training Programs That Build Strong Intergroup Relations on Campus Are More Effective Than Programs That Respond to Specific Incidents of Racism or Campus Crises. There is a tendency on many campuses to launch prejudice reduction programs only after a painful series of racial incidents has occurred. Although this response is understandable and at times appropriate, it may leave others with the false impression that the primary goal of prejudice reduction work is to curtail overt acts of bigotry on campus. An effective prejudice reduction program must strive for much more than just crisis intervention. As Dalton noted in Chapter One, college life offers a unique setting in which human beings from diverse backgrounds can learn how to live together. For many students, their college experiences may be the first and only time that they will live closely with others whom they do not select. The contemporary university can become a model for an increasingly polarized society by developing a deliberate, systematic plan of action that fosters healthy intergroup relations among all members of the campus community.

A related tendency on many campuses has been to view prejudice reduction programs primarily as a tool for managing a public relations problem. Many college administrators have been reluctant to implement programs on welcoming campus diversity, since the establishment of such programs may be perceived as an admission of a serious racial problem (Metz, 1990). As Dalton noted in Chapter One, positive action may indeed generate initial controversy and attention. But the advantages of launching positive, proactive diversity training on campus have often been overlooked. Rather than developing a response under pressure following a racial incident, administrators can foster an academic climate that views the diversity of the campus population as a valued learning resource. The peer training model offers a constructive preventive alternative to crisis intervention.

Programs That Welcome Diversity Need to Include All of the Visible and Invisible Differences Found on Campus. Thomas (1990) claims that those corporations that focused only on African American and white or male and female issues in their diversity awareness programs were less effective than those that addressed a wide range of diversity issues. Racism in the United States, particularly in regard to African Americans, must always be a primary focus of any campus prejudice reduction program. But a major campuswide effort to welcome diversity should include all the many visible and invisible differences among students, including nationality, race, ethnicity, gender, sexual orientation, religious affiliation, physical challenges, age, and socioeconomic class. Many United States students have little understanding of the ways in which their class backgrounds have shaped their view of the world and their interactions with others. Since racism and classism are so closely related, whenever the issues of class are addressed we have observed that the dynamics of racism have been better understood.

One of the more controversial issues in prejudice reduction work on campuses today is whether to address a range of discrimination issues or to focus solely on racism. The concern of many antiracism activities is that the inclusion of other issues can be used as a convenient tactic to avoid the more difficult work on racism. However, the effectiveness of antiracism work can actually be enhanced by including a discussion of other institutionalized forms of discrimination. One of the insidious effects of racism is the isolation experienced by many people of color. A common reaction from many people of color who have participated in the NCBI prejudice reduction programs that include a diverse range of issues is an expression of relief at knowing that they are not the only ones who have experienced serious discrimination. For example, an especially powerful bond among African Americans, gays and lesbians, and Jews often emerges at such training programs (Brown, 1988).

Prejudice Reduction Programs That Are Based on Guilt, Moralizing, or Condemnation Often Rigidify Prejudicial Attitudes. Some students respond negatively—some even with hostility—to prejudice reduction work on campus. It is important not to assume that this reaction is solely the students' fault. Such resistance is often a response to confrontational programs that tend to pressure students into admitting that they are racists. A great challenge in doing antiracism work is to avoid both extremes: If people are targeted and required to label themselves as racist, sexist, and so on, they can become defensive quickly and thereby lost to the work; if the programs are too comfortable, on the other hand, the hard issues never get raised and the unrecognized racism goes unchallenged. Clearly, a proper balance is needed to assist participants to take risks and to raise tough issues without violating their own sense of integrity and self-worth (Brown, 1990).

Antiracism Programs Are Most Effectively Conducted with a Hopeful, Upbeat, Sometimes Even Raucous Tone. The effects of discrimination are serious, and therefore many mistakenly assume that effective antiracism work requires a deadly serious approach. In fact, the most empowering programs, where participants have left eager to fight against institutionalized racism, have always included boisterous cheering and ripping laughter alongside more solemn moments. When people come to a prejudice reduction workshop motivated by fear or painful emotion, they are less able to continue taking powerful leadership. An upbeat tone can pervade all aspects of the program. Bright fliers announcing the workshops are likely to attract greater segments of the campus population; flowers and colorful wall hangings in the workshop environment welcome participants to antiracism work; and the singing together of liberation songs expresses a spirit of joy in challenging oppression.

Theory and Methodology

The NCBI prejudice reduction model was designed to help participants understand the dynamics of institutionalized racism by working through a series of personal and small-group explorations. A close correspondence exists between the theory and the methodology of the workshop model (Mazza, 1989). We will present here the principles governing each component of the model first, followed by the group activity that demonstrates each principle. Mann and Moser, in Chapter Five, examine other models of racial identity development that will also be useful to the reader in considering educational interventions.

Theory: The Formation of Stereotypes. The nature of human intelligence is to store and catalogue similar pieces of information in order to make sense of the surrounding environment. Prejudicial attitudes arise when one takes in misinformation, often in the form of simplistic generalizations, about a particular group. Every distorted piece of information concerning another group is stored as a literal recording, much like a phonograph record. Everything about another group that has ever been heard in casual conversations, read in the newspapers, seen in the cinema, or culled from everyday life forms a part of the recording (Jackins, 1978). Even when subsequent personal experiences contradict the negative recordings, the earlier stored misinformation is not easily erased. Instead, the earlier recordings continue to exert a powerful, often unrecognized influence on thinking and action and may take the form of such generalizations as "all blacks are on welfare," "all gay people are unhappy," or "all Jews are rich." An effective prejudice reduction program will help participants first to identify and then to decrease the influence of the recordings.

Method: First Thoughts. Participants are asked to explore their first thoughts in regard to particular groups. Participants meet in pairs and select an ethnic, racial, gender, or religious group to which neither partner belongs. Choosing a group to which neither participant belongs gives ample permission for participants to learn what recordings are actually stored without first editing the thoughts for fear of offending the partner. With each taking a turn, one partner says the name of the group; the other partner, without hesitation, says his or her first uncensored thoughts. When these thoughts are shared in a large group, it becomes readily apparent that everyone has internalized negative recordings about some group. The advantage of this process is the common discovery that everyone harbors negative recordings; no one person or group is to blame.

Theory: Intragroup Prejudice (Internalized Oppression). Most prejudice reduction programs focus on the stereotypes people have learned about groups other than their own. But one of the most painful results of discrimination is that people may internalize many of these stereotypes and direct them against members of their own group, including themselves. The external criticism becomes a constant internal critique, resulting in members of a group judging harshly anyone in their own group whom they fear might reinforce the negative stereotype. A subtler manifestation of intragroup prejudice is the rigid self-monitored avoidance of particular behavior (for example, women who never allow themselves to express any dependency needs). Intragroup prejudices are a major mechanism for keeping oppressed groups powerless. As long as members of a group deplete their energies by perpetuating internal divisions, they are less likely to rally the power necessary to challenge institutionalized oppression. It is important to help each participant examine the ways in which internalized oppression has kept him or her separate from his or her own group.

Working through intragroup divisions is one prerequisite for building intergroup coalitions. Some may express concern that the exposure of intragroup stereotypes in the presence of others who are not group members will only reinforce negative stereotypes. The authors have found, however, that once people are given the opportunity to witness the painful impact of internalized stereotypes, they gain a deeper appreciation of the heroic struggles of each group in the face of oppression.

Method: Internalized Oppression and Pride. In order to allow participants to examine their own internalized stereotypes, workshop leaders instruct them to meet in pairs and to select a group to which they both belong. Taking turns, each participant points a finger at his or her partner and says, "What I can't stand about you [your own group] is . . . !" For example, a Catholic might say, "What I can't stand about you Catholics is your preoccupation with sin!" An important learning point for participants is that the negative thoughts one has about one's own group are usually derived from the prior negative stereotypes others have had about the group.

Once participants have aired many of the negative feelings toward their own groups, they can then more readily express authentic group pride. Many find that releasing the emotionally charged intragroup stereotypes allows them to overcome any resistance to claiming group pride. Participants return to the same partner, but this time they express what they are proud of concerning their group. For example, the Catholic may say, "What I am most proud of about being Catholic is the global vision of the Church."

Theory: The Extent of Group Oppression. A fundamental tenet of the prejudice reduction model is that human beings have to be mistreated systematically before they will mistreat others (that is, the boss yells at the worker; the worker yells at her son; the son kicks the dog). Therefore, helping every participant to identify and to heal the sources of their own mistreatment is the most effective intervention strategy, since it is directed at the origins rather than at the symptoms of mistreatment.

The most effective communication in groups occurs when each member has a chance to speak and to listen. Often it is impossible to listen to the painful experiences of others unless one is also afforded the opportunity to express one's own painful experiences. When a climate is created that allows every participant to convey important information, there is a mutual investment in listening well. If prejudice reduction workshops resist identifying a hierarchy of oppression (that is, determining which group has been more oppressed), better coalition-building efforts can occur among campus groups. No group issue is too insignificant to be heard. The judgment that one group's experience of mistreatment is not worthy of attention can serve as a wedge that will lead to isolating groups from one another. People may begin dismissing the legitimate concerns of larger and larger numbers of people. An inclusive approach to examining group oppression consolidates, rather than diffuses, support for antiracism work. By listening to each other, groups come to the understanding that their experiences are more similar than they are different, and thus they become willing to work on behalf of each other.

Method: Caucus Reporting. Participants form caucuses of a particular group in which they have experienced injury or discrimination. The list of possible caucuses is proposed by the participants. Caucuses can be formed, for instance, around race, ethnicity, class background, gender, job description, language, sexual orientation, religion, physical characteristics, or any other issue that a participant may suggest. Each caucus is asked to prepare a report, which the caucus then presents to the whole group, responding to the question, "What do you never again want others to say, think, or do toward your group?"

Theory: Attitudinal Change Linked to Sharing Personal Incidents of Discrimination. The most effective communication of the impact of racism is through the sharing of personal stories. People can debate the merits of analytical data concerning the continuing existence of racism; they cannot as easily discount personal experiences of discrimination. Many such personal stories evoke strong emotions in both the teller and the listener. What is consistently surprising about the telling of stories of discrimination is the profound level at which many people are ready to share painful memories. When a person is afforded the rare opportunity to give voice to the experience of injury, the tale commands the group's attention. The stories are always compelling ones, often expressed with considerable personal grief. The telling of personal stories has the unique power to affect attitudinal change (Sales, 1984). Often the listener is stirred to recall parallel experiences that elicit a strong identification with the storyteller. The purpose of personal storytelling is not to reduce all tough intergroup issues to the level of personal counseling. Instead, one of the most effective ways to communicate a universal principle is to present the issue in human terms. Research (Hoffman, 1982; Oliner and Oliner, 1988) emphasizes that one of the key factors that can motivate an individual to work against the oppression of groups is the individual's recognition of a similarity between the oppression of a particular group and incidents of discrimination in his or her own personal history.

The benefits of personal storytelling are not only restricted to the listener. The storyteller also benefits in two principal ways: First, he or she gains a number of new, better-informed allies who are roused to fight against the oppression. Second, he or she is often able to heal the internal pain caused by the original injury. The public sharing of the incident with the attention of a caring group of listeners enables the storyteller to release the emotions that have often been buried since the initial incident. The emotional release is usually experienced as healing.

Method: Speak-Outs. A number of participants are personally invited to "speak out" to the entire group about a specific incident of discrimination. The request is always made privately, aside from the pressure of the group, in order to respect the individual's right to consider the request thoughtfully, to ask any clarifying questions about the process, and to accept or decline the invitation freely. The speak-out format allows the group to focus on the more serious forms of institutionalized oppression that are found on campuses, such as racism, sexism, anti-Semitism, and homophobia. Three or four participants in succession then speak in front of the group, relating a specific incident of discrimination.

Theory: Skill Training for Effective Behavioral Change. One of the key principles of community organizing and empowerment training is that people will gradually reclaim their own power through the achievement of everyday, winnable victories. In training people to claim power in combating racism, we have found that the analogous, everyday, winnable victory in prejudice reduction work is the interruption of oppressive jokes, remarks, and slurs. These comments may not be the most institutionalized forms of discrimination, but they are often the most commonly experienced examples. Sales (1984), professor of applied social research at Boston University, was commissioned by the Institute on American Pluralism of the American Jewish Committee to test the effectiveness of NCBI workshop models on college campuses. Participants in the workshops were tested prior to each workshop and then again six months later. Sales found that participants reported marked shifts in their ability to interrupt oppressive remarks and slurs. Moreover, participants who demonstrated an increased ability to interrupt bigoted remarks were also demonstrating an increased ability to initiate efforts to eradicate institutionalized racism. Feelings of powerlessness underlie the reluctance of many people to work against racism. Providing students, faculty, and administrators with practical skills that give them even a small sense of control over their environment is the first step toward achieving greater institutional changes.

When most people hear oppressive comments, they tend to respond in one of two ways. They either freeze and say nothing, or they respond with self-righteous condemnation (for example, "Don't you ever say that again around me!"). Neither response is effective in achieving attitudinal change. The first tactic is a retreat: The person making the bigoted remark goes unchallenged, and the person hearing the remark withdraws into self-reproach. The second tactic is counterproductive: The person making the bigoted comment is put into a defensive stance, unable to hear new information; the person responding to the remark may feel empowered but mistakes a rebuke for an effective intervention. In order to be effective, one must understand the psychological dynamics driving bigoted comments.

There are three principles informing our skill training efforts to affect behavioral change regarding oppressive comments. First, we debunk the strangely consoling myth of "unreachable" bigots, a distinctive group—fundamentally different—who are responsible for perpetuating the varied forms of discrimination. With this myth in place, the unsettling broader picture is rarely considered—that is, that all of us harbor prejudices. A portion of one's self-righteous condemnation in reaction to another's bigoted comment may be traced to one's own insecurity. It is often easier to condemn another person than it is to face one's own prejudicial attitudes.

Painful as it may be, an effective strategy for antiracism intervention is built on finding a common humanity with those who express bigotry.

Second, it is useful to adopt the attitude toward people who are making prejudicial remarks that their comments are a call for help. So much attention is diverted to stopping an offensive comment at all cost that little consideration is given to the underlying forces generating the behavior. Expressions of bigotry have their origins in recordings of fear or injury. To stop a person from saying a bigoted comment may curtail an isolated effect, but it does not address the underlying cause, the recordings that fuel the comments. Such recordings are healed by airing them. Instead of quickly acting to silence a person who makes a bigoted comment, a more effective strategy is to employ a range of techniques that are designed to assist the healing of recordings (such as humor, careful listening, and respectful questions).

Third, the principle obstacle in thinking creatively about how to heal the prejudicial recordings of others is that their comments often trigger our own painful experiences and thereby confound clear thinking. In order to be able to assist another person, we must first give attention to healing our own painful experiences. If a person has already released and healed the hostile feelings that oppressive comments evoke, he or she is more apt to produce a number of creative responses.

Method: Role-Plays on How to Interrupt Bigoted Comments. Participants generate a list of bigoted jokes, remarks, and slurs most frequently heard on campus. A representative sample is selected for demonstration in front of the large group. A participant is invited to come up in front of the group in order to work on the particular offensive comment he or she has heard. First, in order to heal the blocks to effective thinking, the participant is encouraged to vent his or her strong feelings evoked by the comment. Then, the original situation is role-played with the participant being coached to experiment with a range of effective responses.

Theory: The Ability to Handle Intergroup Conflict. Most antiracism training programs emphasize the reduction of bigoted attitudes and behaviors. But working to change attitudes, though essential, is not sufficient for building a diverse campus community. Students, faculty, and administrators need to learn specific intergroup conflict resolution skills. There are many highly emotional, politicized issues in campus life: legalization of drugs, abortion, banning private societies on campus, euthanasia, mandated prejudice reduction programs, sanctions against South Africa, affirmative action programs, and banning controversial speakers. Principled people often hold opposing positions on these issues; legitimate differences, however, all too often lead to misunderstanding, tension, and intergroup polarization. Welcoming diversity on campus must include the skill of coalition building: the ability to bring disparate groups together in order to identify and work toward common goals. Many campus leaders all too readily become advocates, poised to fight for their own points of view. Effective peer leaders for prejudice reduction on campus are those who can articulate heartfelt concerns on all sides of a controversial issue and build bridges among discordant groups (Brown, 1984).

Method: Intergroup Conflict Process. Participants select a controversial, emotionally charged political issue that can be framed in terms of a pro or con position. A spokesperson from each side of the issue is invited to speak in front of the group. After each spokesperson explains his or her position, the other spokesperson repeats back with as much accuracy as possible what he or she heard. Next, each spokesperson has a chance to ask a clarifying question that will gather new information about the position of the other. The skill of asking a question that will bring new information to the surface and serve to move the discussion forward is a hard one to learn. Such questions can only be entertained when one is willing to consider that new information may lead to a revision of one's own initial position.

After each spokesperson has been given an opportunity to present the issue to his or her satisfaction, a written list is assembled of the arguments advanced both for and against each position. Participants meet in pairs first to consider what both sides have in common and then to consider a way to reframe the original question in light of their shared interests. The process involves the entire group in joint problem solving, moving from terms of exclusive position taking to exploring avenues of mutual concern.

Developing the Team of Peer Trainers

Teams trained in our prejudice reduction models are currently functioning on twenty college campuses. Preparing for the long-term success of these teams involves a four-stage implementation process (Oliver and Slavin, 1989).

Stage 1: Developing the Campus Leadership Team. A three- to five-person campus leadership team, composed of students, faculty, and administrators, first receives training. One to six months prior to launching the campus peer training program, the campus leadership team attends one of the semiannual NCBI international trainers' institutes conducted in Boston. Participating together in the trainers' institute affords the leadership team an opportunity to establish a cooperative working relationship as the team members learn together how to lead prejudice reduction workshops. After returning to the campus, they are able to work with each other in practicing the workshop techniques and adjusting the training to respond to the unique needs of their campus. A chairperson is selected from among the members of the campus leadership team in order to facilitate contact with NCBI and to convene local meetings.

Stage 2: Holding the Peer Training Seminar. The campus leadership team recruits twenty-five to fifty participants for a three-day peer training seminar conducted by NCBI staff. The participants are selected from a diverse cross section of the campus community, including student leaders (especially returning sophomores and juniors), administrators, faculty, support staff, and campus police. It is important to seek representatives of a range of different cultural and religious groups, as well as men and women and persons with disabilities. A prerequisite for participation in the training is an explicit commitment from each participant to lead a number of campus prejudice reduction workshops in the coming year.

All of the components of this prejudice reduction model are taught during the first two days. The third day is devoted to responding to the difficulties that participants anticipate in leading workshops on campus. Each participant is offered an opportunity for individual coaching in order to address his or her personal concerns.

The members of the campus leadership team function as leaders of small-group practice sessions during the peer training seminar. Four or five times during the training, they convene small groups where participants have an opportunity to practice leading various parts of the prejudice reduction model and to receive supervision, feedback, and encouragement.

Stage 3: Maintaining an Ongoing Support Group. Following the peer training seminar, the chairperson of the campus leadership team convenes and leads regular support-group sessions for all of the peer trainers.

Meetings of the support group serve a twofold purpose. First, they give all the peer trainers a safe place in which to continue honing their prejudice reduction leadership skills. A key component in the success of our campus work is providing an opportunity for peer trainers to identify and to heal the emotional blocks that hinder them in leading workshops. Their prior training helps the members of the campus leadership team to assist the peer trainers in developing their leadership. The support-group meetings engender a spirit of camaraderie. The peer trainers are moved by each other's speak-outs; they cheer each other on in leading parts of the workshop model; and they develop a deeper, mutual commitment to the success of the program.

Second, the support-group meetings enable the peer trainers to set new goals and strategies with an eye to effecting long-term change on campus.

Stage 4: Conducting Follow-up Training and Supervision. We believe it is important for the campus leadership team to participate in an advanced NCBI workshop six months after the initial peer training seminar on campus. This advanced consultation helps team members to review the status of the campuswide effort. Supervision sessions also provide them with additional individual coaching in any area of concern that may have arisen while they conducted campus programs.

To offer ongoing support and supervision to these peer campus teams, NCBI recently launched a Campus Affiliate Program. Through this program, each team leader receives bimonthly phone consultation, an affiliate training manual with how-to tips on facilitating effective team meetings, and a biannual newsletter highlighting effective prejudice reduction programs on other campuses.

The Long-Range Impact of Peer Training

The impact of the antiracism work offered by campus peer training teams extends far beyond an annual prejudice reduction workshop. Peer training is part of a larger institutional response to racism. On a number of college campuses, every student participates in several welcoming-diversity workshops each year; similarly, programs have been held for student organizations, senior administrators, and faculty members. The peer workshops promote an increased sense of well-being in the campus community. Many students, faculty, and administrators who never spoke to one another prior to the trainings establish a mutual commitment to improve campus life.

The peer training team functions as a significant campus resource in two ways. First, the group members can be called on during campus crises to play a mediating role. Second, they can provide invaluable consultation to college administrators in formulating campus policies on diversity issues. As colleges and universities continue to attract a diverse population in the next decade, the need for prejudice reduction peer training teams that can teach campuses how to welcome diversity will undoubtedly increase.

References

Brown, C. R. *The Art of Coalition Building: A Guide for Community Leaders.* New York: American Jewish Committee, 1984.

Brown, C. R. "Black-Jewish Relations." Paper presented at the Tikkun Conference, New York, December 20, 1988.

Brown, C. R. "The Community Leader as Coalition Builder: Building an Intergroup Relations Movement in South Africa." Paper presented at the Twenty-Fifth Anniversary Conference of the University of Port Elizabeth, South Africa, February 15, 1990.

Hoffman, M. L. "Development of Prosocial Motivation: Empathy and Guilt." In N. Eisenberg (ed.), *Development of Prosocial Behavior.* New York: Academic Press, 1982.

Jackins, H. *The Human Side of Human Beings: The Theory of Reevaluation Counseling.* Seattle, Wash.: Rational Island Press, 1978.

Mazza, G. J. "Dealing with Emotional Content in Negotiation: The National Coalition-Building Institute Methodology." Paper presented at the Kennedy School of Government at Harvard University, Cambridge, Massachusetts, May 15, 1989.

Metz, H. "Bad Apples, Evil Deeds: How Law Students Deface Free Speech." *Student Lawyer,* 1990, *18* (6), 33–38.

Oliner, S. P., and Oliner, P. M. *The Altruistic Personality*. New York: Free Press, 1988.

Oliver, E. A., and Slavin, D. "The NCBI Prejudice Reduction Model: A Process for Building a Multicultural Campus Community." *CUPA Journal*, 1989, *40* (3), 44–47.

Sales, A. *The Effectiveness of NCBI Workshop Models*. New York: Institute of American Pluralism, American Jewish Committee, 1984.

Smith, D. C. "Righting the Wrongs of Racism." *Christian Science Monitor*, October 23, 1989, p. 14.

Thomas, R. R., Jr. "From Affirmative Action to Affirming Diversity." *Harvard Business Review*, 1990, *68* (2), 107–117.

Cherie R. Brown is executive director of the National Coalition Building Institute in Arlington, Massachusetts.

George J. Mazza has been an NCBI associate since 1985 and has applied peer training techniques to his work with religious organizations.

A theoretical framework is presented to suggest ways of designing peer intervention programs and of grouping existing programs.

A Model for Designing Peer-Initiated Activities to Promote Racial Awareness and an Appreciation of Differences

Barbara A. Mann, Rita M. Moser

Previous chapters have examined the problem of bias in college peer culture, African American and white student interactions on campus, and racial differences in student experiences and attitudes. A common theme of these chapters is the importance of understanding the influence of peer groups on college students' social attitudes and behaviors. Student-initiated activities among peers can be one of the most powerful influences for changing racial and ethnic stereotypes and behaviors. This chapter presents a theoretical framework for designing peer interventions, suggests criteria for effective racial awareness programs, and discusses examples of successful college prejudice reduction activities.

A Range of Theoretical Frameworks

College students differ in their general levels of racial and ethnic awareness, and on a given campus, students will exhibit different levels of awareness and acceptance of diversity. Student developmental theory provides student affairs practitioners with the framework needed to plan effective interventions that will target the conditions found on their particular campuses. Knefelkamp and Golec (1985) state that "we can use theory as a framework—to inform thinking, for assessment and program design, and to assess environments as well as persons. To do so, we need to modify and adapt theory to our particular students and our particular environmental context" (p. 5). Programmatic efforts should, therefore, be chosen after an adequate assessment of student needs and readiness levels and should be supported by a theoretical framework suitable for the campus situation.

Several models and theories are available to assist with an understanding of campus tolerance for diversity and individual development as it relates to racial and ethnic diversity (Ashley, 1990; Chasteen, 1990; Haan, Aerts, and Cooper, 1985; Hughes, 1987; Jackson and Hardiman, 1988; Katz, 1978; Sedlacek and Brooks, 1976). This chapter discusses and integrates two theoretical models. One model focuses on achieving an appreciation of diversity in the campus environment; the other addresses developmental issues in individual racial identity. Both theories are utilized to create a conceptual framework for choosing effective peer interventions.

A Campus Diversity Model

Hughes (1987) suggests that there are six developmental stages that characterize different racial awareness levels in campus groups: (1) valuing diversity negatively; (2) exploring the meaning of diversity and creating learning opportunities; (3) gaining acceptance and increasing tolerance for diversity; (4) testing principles of diversity in creative ways; (5) valuing diversity positively; and (6) building the human community. These stages and the attitudes and behavior that characterize them can be used to determine the level of racial awareness of campus populations and of target groups and to design and select educational interventions to promote awareness and development. Programming interventions are most effective when they target the appropriate developmental stages found in the campus community.

Racial Identity Models

Racial identity models, summarized by Helms (1990) can be used as a framework for programmatic intervention based on the assumption "that interracial conflict has personal racial identity developmental issues as its source, and therefore, if interracial communication is to be encouraged, then the individual must first come to understand her or his own racial identity issues" (p. 206). To help students achieve this understanding, two similar and useful racial identity models of stage development are available for the practitioner. Helms proposes a model of white racial identity development consisting of two phases: Phase one, the abandonment of racism, consists of the three stages of contact, disintegration, and reintegration; and phase two, defining a nonracist white identity, consists of the three stages of pseudoindependence, immersion and emersion, and autonomy. Jackson and Hardiman (1988), on the other hand, propose a five-stage white racial identity model based on unlearning oppressive attitudes and behaviors.

Both models emphasize the development of a positive white racial identity that "involves an awareness of personal responsibility for racism, consistent acknowledgment of one's whiteness, and abandonment of racism in any of its forms as a defining aspect of one's personality" (Helms, 1990, p. 53).

Helms points out that "the primary difference in the two models was that Hardiman placed more emphasis on racism as the catalyst for identity development whereas Helms placed more emphasis on moral dilemmas in social interactions" (p. 67). Since the emphasis in this chapter is on campus peer interventions, we use the Jackson and Hardiman (1988) model, which has been utilized extensively on a college campus as the basis for understanding how to reduce racism and how to foster an appreciation of differences.

People learn their behaviors, actions, attitudes, and beliefs regarding racial issues as children. Once oppressive structures are in place, Jackson and Hardiman (1988) believe that "oppression becomes normalized, and succeeding generations of oppressors learn to accept their inheritance of oppression as normal, the way things are and always will be, the natural order to things" (p. 6).

The learning and unlearning process for both the oppressor and the oppressed can be described in a sequence of developmental stages that can serve as a diagnostic and intervention planning tool in antioppression education. The Jackson and Hardiman Oppression/Liberation Development Model (OLDM) combines what is known about social identity development processes for individuals and groups with what is known about effects that specific manifestations of oppression have on individual and group development. The OLDM describes the process that oppressor and oppressed move through in the struggle to attain a liberated social identity in an oppressive environment.

The OLDM's five stages, outlined in Figure 5.1, range from an oppressive or oppressed consciousness to a liberated social consciousness for white or African American persons. The authors identify the stages as (1) naiveté, (2) acceptance, (3) resistance, (4) redefinition, and (5) internalization. The stages of acceptance and resistance have two possible manifestations: passive (unconscious) or active (conscious).

The transition from one stage to another is typically motivated by a recognition that one's current worldview is either illogical, detrimental to a healthy self-concept, impractical, or in general no longer serves some important self-interest. During the transition period, a person or group may appear to themselves and to others to be in two stages simultaneously. This results from being in the exit phase of one stage and the entry phase of the next stage at the same time. Although the OLDM's stages of racial identity development are the same for African Americans and whites, the experiences they go through within each stage are understandably different. For our purposes, we shall examine the application of the racial identity model to stages of development for whites.

Stage One: Naiveté. All individuals are born without social consciousness and are taught social group memberships and social status by powerful

Figure 5.1. Stages of Racial Identity Development

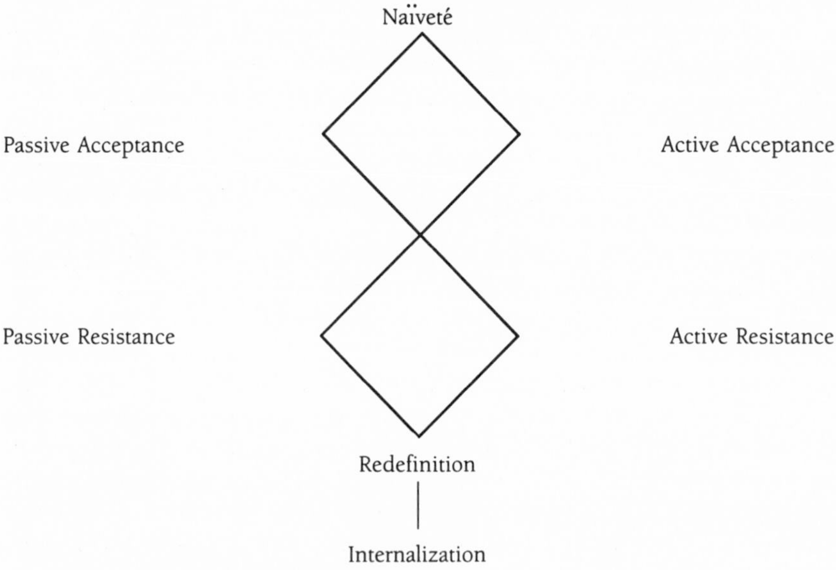

Naïveté

Passive Acceptance   Active Acceptance

Passive Resistance   Active Resistance

Redefinition

Internalization

Source: Adapted from Jackson and Hardiman, 1983.

socializers such as parents and peers. The messages a person receives "are usually a mixture of truths and falsehoods about their social group membership, what is right and natural, and what is wrong and deviant" (Jackson and Hardiman, 1988, p. 17). Since this stage generally ends at about age four, this chapter focuses on the succeeding stages.

Stage Two: Acceptance. In the *active* stage of acceptance, whites consciously identify with the social system that gives them certain privileges based on their race. They operate on and actively disseminate negative stereotypes about oppressed groups, such as the belief that minorities possess genetic and biological inferiorities. Whites blame oppressed people for their oppressed condition. They reward those who support the oppressive logic system and punish those who question or challenge the system. Toward the end of this stage, people begin to recognize that some of the challenges to the current system may have some validity. They begin to question the espoused rightness of the oppressive system.

Individuals in the *passive* stage unconsciously identify with the social system and the social group that gives them privilege. Passives typically deny the existence of social oppression and blame the oppressed for their condition. They agree to help the oppressed overcome their self-made condition so that they will fit into the oppressor's system, thereby acting out a form of paternalistic helping. Toward the end of this stage, they begin to acknowledge that there are some injustices in society and that the oppressed group's condition may not be all its own doing. Many individuals fail to move beyond the acceptance stage.

Behaviors that are typical of this stage may include avoidance of contact with persons of color or deferential treatment in a patronizing manner; hiring persons of color for support positions but not trusting them in leadership roles; and accepting or actively supporting racist jokes, language, rumors, and assumptions. Indicators of beliefs at the acceptance stage may include such statements as "affirmative action is reverse discrimination; it gives unfair advantages to minorities that whites never had"; "minorities need special training so they can fit into the way the campus operates"; and "everyone has an equal chance to succeed if they just work hard and don't rock the boat" (Jackson and Hardiman, 1983, p. 115). One can see these beliefs and attitudes expressed by members of white student unions, described by Dalton in Chapter One.

Stage Three: Resistance. A person in the *active* stage of resistance questions the social support for oppression. Challenging oppression whenever it is identified in people or institutions is a typical behavior. Individuals in this stage own their oppressive behavior and their implicit support for oppressive institutions. They feel shame, guilt, and anger over the existence of oppression and their role in maintaining it.

At the end of this stage, individuals actively reject their own oppressive behavior and attitudes and the social systems that teach and support oppression. They actively reject the privilege gained from an oppressive system and begin to experience an identity void and a need to redefine the self.

A person in the *passive* stage of resistance searches for examples of oppression in the behavior of individuals and institutions. Questioning and challenging the existence of oppression in socially and professionally safe situations is typical. The person recognizes the existence of oppression and its pervasiveness throughout society. This recognition often results in an attempt to drop out or distance oneself from the social system. The frustration that results from this alienation often causes the person to engage more actively in examining the problem. The person will then usually begin by owning his or her own participation in the oppressive system and by rejecting the tenets of that system. Like the person at the final level of active resistance, this person begins to ask, "Who am I?"

Behaviors typical of this stage can include challenging racist jokes and comments by white co-workers; trying to learn more about personal racism and systemic racism; and becoming active in campus committees or organizations that focus on equal employment opportunity, affirmative action, or interracial projects. Belief statements typical of the resistance stage can include "racism is a pervasive force in American society"; "minorities have the deck stacked against them in organizations despite affirmative action"; and "whites are responsible for maintaining and supporting racism" (Jackson and Hardiman, 1983, p. 116).

Stage Four: Redefinition. The effort to answer the question "Who am I?" takes the person at this stage on a search for new ways to define his or her social group and his or her membership in that social group. The process of searching, investigating, observing, and engaging in dialogue with other members of the same social group results in a new social identity. The task of stage four, then, is to develop a sense of social identity within a person's own group that is positive and affirming.

Behaviors typical of the redefinition stage may include trying to help white peers become more sensitive to racism and to their racial identity, working more with whites on addressing their racism and less on giving "help" to persons of color, and examining the white culture and developing an awareness of its strengths and limitations. Statements indicative of beliefs in the redefinition stage can include "whites are responsible for working with other whites on eradicating racism"; "organizations must continually grapple with the integration of multicultural perspectives for their own success and effectiveness"; and "organizations' norms, policies, and structures benefit white employees and alienate minority employees" (Jackson and Hardiman, 1983, p. 117).

Stage Five: Internalization. Individuals at this stage, aware of their past and concerned about creating the future, apply and integrate their new social identity into all other aspects of their identity. As the individual becomes more comfortable with the application of the new identity, this new identity becomes internalized. Once internalized, the new identity must be nurtured in order to be sustained in a hostile environment and to resist new and improved attempts to resocialize it into the oppressive society. This stage is characterized by the person becoming knowledgeable about racial, cultural, and sexual orientation similarities. The person accepts, respects, and appreciates both minority and majority individuals.

Behaviors of individuals at the internalization stage include interacting authentically with members of all racial groups, regardless of their stage of consciousness; attempting to integrate all cultural perspectives into the organization's operations; and continuing to work on confronting racism on the campus from a redefined white perspective. Statements that are indicators of the internalization stage include "organizations can benefit from the diversity of perspectives of different racial groups"; "I recognize, appreciate, and affirm my own race and other races without idealizing or deprecating"; and "I see the connection between racism and other forms of oppression" (Jackson and Hardiman, 1983, p. 118).

Implications of the OLDM Model. The OLDM model can serve as a basis for assessing the developmental levels of individuals and groups. It can serve as a planning and teaching tool for student affairs practitioners confronting racism. Peer-initiated interventions based on this model can be particularly powerful given the importance of the peer group in the socialization of college students.

Integrating the Models

Knefelkamp and Golec (1985) state that "we need to use theories in combination with one another in order to obtain a more complex and adequate view of our clients" (p. 5). Thus, the OLDM model helps to demonstrate how individuals can move toward building the multicultural community described by Hughes (1987). Table 5.1 illustrates the interrelationship of the stages of the two models. The combined models help to clarify the developmental levels to which particular interventions apply.

Choosing Effective Interventions

Selecting effective programmatic interventions requires an assessment of the targeted population. If campuswide programs are planned, then one must look at several factors about the campus climate to gauge what kinds of programs may be most effective in promoting racial awareness. Specific campus conditions have either favorable or unfavorable effects on race relations and must be considered in designing educational interventions.

The number of African American students on a predominantly white campus, their retention and comfort level at the institution, and their relationships with majority students are important factors in determining appropriate interventions. Consider a campus where minority students are present in higher proportions, where they are more effectively retained, and where they are represented in the campus leadership structure. If minority and majority students alike have strong ownership and involvement in the same activities and organizations, then this campus is likely to have some success with peer-initiated efforts to promote an appreciation of differences.

Table 5.1. Integrating the Campus Diversity Model and the Racial Identity Model

Campus Diversity Model (Hughes)	Racial Identity Model (Jackson and Hardiman)
Developmental levels of diversity	Stages of racial identity
Valuing diversity negatively	Acceptance
Exploring the meaning of diversity and creating learning opportunities	Resistance
Gaining acceptance and increasing tolerance for diversity	Resistance
Testing principles of diversity in creative ways	Redefinition
Valuing diversity positively	Internalization
Building the human community	Internalization

On the other hand, a predominantly white campus with a small proportion of African American students whose retention and involvement are marginal is more likely to require structured programs that encourage majority students to value differences and discourage prejudicial attitudes and behaviors. The campus will also need to strategize ways to motivate African American students to take a more active role in the campus community. Focusing on developing a positive climate by creating a strong organization for African American students may assist in raising their comfort level on that campus.

Movement from structured programs planned by administrators and faculty toward peer-initiated efforts will be more effective when the students have reached level two of the Hughes model. At this point, participants are "willing, perhaps eager, to learn about diverse cultures and groups" (Hughes, 1987, p. 544). This stage compares to the resistance stage of the Oppression/Liberation Development Model (Jackson and Hardiman, 1988). This is also the stage in which programs can best be planned for joint participation by African American and white students.

Based on the Hughes model and the Oppression/Liberation Development Model, one can conclude that as student groups become more appreciative of racial and ethnic differences and more motivated to support these differences, the groups can be powerful catalysts for change with their peers. As their own growth proceeds, group members will be increasingly prepared to assume responsibility for helping others to change as well.

Students who have reached the fourth stage, redefinition, will be much more effective peer leaders. They will have passed the more emotionally laden stage of resistance. Their motives for promoting racial awareness and an appreciation of differences will be based on understanding rather than on anger or frustration with society.

Selected Peer Intervention Models

The programs presented here are among those that are currently in place in colleges and universities to promote racial awareness and an appreciation of differences. Each is described and categorized in terms of the stage of the Oppression/Liberation Development Model that it addresses.

Awareness Level: Acceptance. The Acceptance Level can be illustrated by programs initiated on several college campuses.

Hate Busters, William Jewell College. Hate Busters is a student organization formed by Ed Chasteen (1990), who teaches race relations at William Jewell College in Liberty, Missouri. Through the students' academic study of race relations and cultural anthropology, they learn how racial bigotry, religious intolerance, and cultural conflict damage individuals, communities, and societies. As they learn, the students pledge themselves to resist hate in all its forms—bigotry, prejudice, discrimination, intolerance, racism, sexism, ageism, and nationalism—and they pledge to resist hate groups. As part of their pledge, the students will "go anywhere at any time" to help people "settle their differences and live peaceably and productively together" (Chasteen, 1990, p. 139).

This model concentrates on perfecting the worldview of individuals. Each person is the sum of his or her experience and incorporates segments of that experience. To perfect this private world out of which individuals make decisions that direct the public self, the model uses three steps: Learn to like yourself, learn to like those who are like yourself, and learn to like those who are not like yourself. As the Hate Busters confront racism, they assist others in taking these three steps to altering their worldviews.

Racial Awareness Pilot Project and RAPPORT, University of Cincinnati. The Racial Awareness Pilot Project (RAPP) is a selective program that provides a yearlong discussion group where students can explore issues of racial awareness (Division of Undergraduate Studies and Student Affairs, 1990). This student-run program selects group members from among those expressing an interest, paying attention in the selection process to balancing gender, race, academic majors, and level of involvement in campus organizations. After an initial assessment of racial attitudes and identity levels, members attend an orientation dinner and participate in a discussion after viewing the movie *Soul Man.* This is followed by participation in a daylong workshop on race relations. The workshop raises challenging questions about the students' acceptance of racism, and students begin the long process of reexamining their own attitudes. The RAPP participants also have required reading assignments and keep a journal throughout the year. The group members hold biweekly discussions, see movies, attend cultural events, sponsor programs open to everyone on campus, and talk about personal feelings. Staff support is available to individuals as well as to the group as members work through their levels of development.

RAPPORT, composed of RAPP alumni, conducts educational programs both on and off the campus. RAPPORT members have been involved in student government retreats, programming in residence halls, and training student orientation and fraternity and sorority leaders. As a result of their experience with RAPPORT, the student government instituted the Racial Awareness Discussion Sessions (RADS) for all its executive officers, senators, and cabinet directors.

RAPP has served as the inspiration for a variety of strategies and programs to enhance racial awareness on other campuses. These programs include RAPP, at Cornell University; the Racial Awareness and Sensitivity Program (RASP), at Ohio State University; Students Talking About Racial Tolerance (START), also at Ohio State University; and Racial Awareness: A Cooperative Effort (RACE), at the University of Dayton. The RAPP model confronts students in the acceptance stage and those in the early resistance stage, as do the models that follow.

Racism Improvisational Group, Towson State University. The Racism Improvisational Group takes the subtle acts of racism that often occur on college campuses and weaves them into a series of vignettes that serve as catalysts for discussion. The improvisations originated out of planning for a forum on campus violence. Students involved in the planning decided to form a group that would act out some of the subtle forms of racism they had experienced on campus. The vignettes tell the story of racism's effects and encourage an emotional response from the audience. The actors report they are more aware of racism as a result of their experiences ("Group Attacks Racism Through Improvisation," 1990).

Students Together Against Racial Separation (STARS), University of Virginia. As Bourassa describes in Chapter Two, STARS is a grass-roots student group initiated by an ethnically mixed group of residence hall students who were concerned about the degree of racial separatism they encountered. STARS provides a range of planned events and informal discussions (Ponterotto, Grieger, and Heaphy, 1985).

Awareness Level: Resistance. The Resistance Level is well illustrated by a student-initiated program in Washington, D.C.

District of Columbia Student Coalition Against Apartheid and Racism (D.C.SCAR). This group is a regional, multiracial, nonprofit coalition of active students and youth concerned with educational equality, apartheid in South Africa, and the detrimental effects of racism and bias in a multicultural society. Their primary focus has been "to educate its members and fellow students about the system of apartheid in South Africa, the effects of racism in the U.S., and effective means of challenging both" ("D.C. SCAR Hosts National Racism Conference," 1990, p. 2). D.C.SCAR members come from universities in the Washington, D.C., metropolitan area, from local high schools, and from the community at large. The coalition believes that when one group, be it a majority or minority, determines the monocultural norms of a society, there will be racial tension, discrimination, alienation, and perpetual inequality. They stand for the ideal of a multicultural society in which there is mutual and sincere respect for the history and cultural distinctions of various racial and ethnic communities (D.C. Student Coalition Against Apartheid and Racism, 1990).

D.C.SCAR serves as an organizing center for antiracist and antiapartheid activity; it conducts bimonthly meetings, workshops, and presentations and cosponsors area mobilizations, education events, and direct actions. The organization publishes *SCAR News,* a national student newspaper on racism, South Africa, and student activism. Other activities have included participating in the University of Maryland's divestment struggle, fighting for comprehensive sanctions against South Africa, working with Howard University students in the aftermath of the student-police activities in Virginia Beach in 1989, and holding national student conferences on issues related to racism.

Institutions that have organizations affiliated with D.C.SCAR include American University, Catholic University, George Mason University, George Washington University, Georgetown University, Howard University, Montgomery Community College, Northern Virginia Community College, the University of the District of Columbia, and the University of Maryland. These institutions challenge and promote involvement of students in the acceptance and resistance stages.

Awareness Level: Redefinition. The University of Texas, Austin, has a program in place that illustrates the Redefinition Level.

University of Texas, Austin, Multicultural Program. The Dean of Students Office and the Students' Association at the University of Texas, Austin, established a multicultural program for all incoming undergraduate students as part of the summer orientation program. The purpose of the program, led by a group of trained peer facilitators, was to acquaint freshmen with the opportunities and challenges of a culturally diverse campus. The program was designed to sensitize students in the acceptance and resistance stages, but it is most effective with students in the redefinition stage who are searching for ways to express their new understandings and incorporate them into their actions.

The students attending the orientation program view a twenty-minute segment of the Public Broadcasting System special "A Class Divided," which documents an exercise with third-graders about discrimination based on eye color. The freshmen are then divided into small groups for discussions led by the peer facilitators. These sessions address a series of questions focusing on the new students' reactions to the video. Common stereotypes, racial myths, and issues of discrimination are subjects for discussion. The students then receive a multicultural resource guide prepared by a group of students and by the dean of students staff.

Key to the program is the skill of the peer facilitators. These students undergo a training program designed to prepare them to facilitate the discussion and to handle potential problems. Appropriate questions for the program are generated, and a short lecture on the value of diversity is prepared. The students are provided with a written guide containing tips for facilitating discussion. The peer facilitators report that many new students are not necessarily hateful or racist but are misinformed. The program helps the new students to think about today's issues and gives them a framework in which to consider them. The peer facilitators report that the entire project is educational for themselves and sensitizes them to issues of racism and diversity (Trevino, 1990).

Awareness Level: Internalization. In the internalization stage, individuals find ways to build bridges between themselves and the persons and organizations around them. Rather than acting as barriers to communication, the individuals' new identities are open to diverse and multicultural social discourse, particularly on a college campus. At this stage, the campus is building the human community as described by Hughes (1987).

Celebrating Our World, University of Wisconsin, Whitewater. The Celebrating Our World (COW) committee is an example of a peer intervention strategy that works particularly well for students at the internalization stage. The committee combats oppression through the promotion of antioppression activities. The COW mission statement articulates the students' beliefs: "I celebrate my sisters and brothers who are the colors of the rainbow. I celebrate those who are physically different than me. I celebrate the spectrum of sexual orientations. I celebrate those who are citizens of countries around the world. I celebrate the different spiritual powers that give us guidance and comfort. I'm proud to celebrate diversity. Won't you join me in celebrating our world?" (University of Wisconsin, 1990).

The COW committee plans an annual week of educational events offered to the campus community to foster an understanding and respect for human diversity. The goals of these events include affirming the worth of individuals (for example, through a program on self-esteem), celebrating the richness of diversity (through an international-food-tasting night and an entertainment night), promoting self-education (through a miniconference that features several speakers), asserting the importance of caring (as shown in an AIDS education dance marathon fund raiser), and reaching out to grade school children to discuss and promote a celebration of diversity.

Conclusion

Some of the peer interventions presented here were initiated by peers and others were initiated by staff in the formative stages. What the programs have in common, though, is the involvement of students at the grass-roots level. Staff may serve as the original organizers or as continuing consultants and trainers, but the students are responsible for maintaining the organization. This substantial involvement of students ensures a peer focus to these interventions. Just as racism is learned through group membership, it can be unlearned on a campus with a peer culture that values diversity and the human community. Each of these peer interventions also enjoys institutional support through recognition, full or partial financing, and institutional commitment. Most are one part of a larger campus effort to promote racial awareness and an appreciation of differences.

The students involved in the peer interventions mention the impact of the activity on their own views. If the students are not already at the redefinition stage of the OLDM, they quickly reach that level through their involvement and begin to work on the internalization stage. The peer intervention activities provide the means by which they can internalize their new knowledge, understanding, and appreciation of the human community.

Efforts to educate for diversity are more likely to be successful when they are based on a theoretical model that recognizes the developmental stages of students as well as the developmental stage of the campus and of various target groups as a whole. The integrated theoretical model set forth in this chapter suggests that the positive valuing of diversity can be merely an intellectual exercise for some students if their own underlying racial identity issues have not yet been thoroughly explored. Other theoretical models of racial identity development are available in the professional literature and can be used to plan a total racial awareness program and target peer interventions.

References

Ashley, M. E. *Combating Racism on Campus.* Cincinnati, Ohio: Division of Undergraduate and Student Affairs, University of Cincinnati, 1990.

Chasteen, E. *How to Like People Who Are Not Like You.* Liberty, Mo.: Amity Books, 1990.

"D.C. SCAR Hosts National Racism Conference." *SCAR News,* June 1990, pp. 1–13.

D.C. Student Coalition Against Apartheid and Racism (D.C. SCAR). *D.C. SCAR: The D.C. Student Coalition Against Apartheid and Racism.* Washington, D.C.: D.C. SCAR, 1990.

Division of Undergraduate Studies and Student Affairs, University of Cincinnati. *UC RAPPs,* Spring 1990 (entire issue).

"Group Attacks Racism Through Improvisation." *National On-Campus Report,* April 2, 1990, pp. 1–2.

Haan, N., Aerts, E., and Cooper, B. *On Moral Grounds: The Search for Practical Morality.* New York: New York University Press, 1985.

Helms, J. E. (ed.). *Black and White Racial Identity: Theory, Research, and Practice.* New York: Greenwood Press, 1990.

Hughes, M. S. "Black Students' Participation in Higher Education." *Journal of College Student Personnel,* 1987, 28 (6), 532–545.

Jackson, B. W., and Hardiman, R. "Racial Identity Development: Implications for Managing the Multicultural Work Force." In R. A. Ritvo and A. F. Sargent (eds.), *The NTL Manager's Handbook.* Arlington, Va.: National Training Laboratory Institute, 1983.

Jackson, B. W., and Hardiman, R. "Oppression: Conceptual and Developmental Analysis." In M. Adams and L. Marchesani (eds.), *Racial and Cultural Diversity, Curricular Content, and Classroom Dynamics: A Manual for College Teachers.* Amherst: University of Massachusetts, 1988.

Katz, J. H. *White Awareness: Handbook for Antiracism Training.* Norman: University of Oklahoma Press, 1978.

Knefelkamp, L. L., and Golec, R. R. *A Workbook for Using the PTP Model.* College Park: University of Maryland, 1985.

Ponterotto, J. G., Grieger, I., and Heaphy, T. J. "Students Together Against Racial Separatism." *Journal of College Student Personnel,* 1985, 26, 251–253.

Sedlacek, W. E., and Brooks, G. C., Jr. *Racism in American Education: A Model for Change.* Chicago: Nelson-Hall, 1976.

Trevino, C. *From Dream to Reality: Multicultural Programming for the Nineties.* Paper presented at the meeting of the National Association for Student Personnel Administrators, New Orleans, March 15, 1990.

University of Wisconsin. *The First Step.* Whitewater: University of Wisconsin, 1990.

Barbara A. Mann is associate professor of higher education at Florida State University.

Rita M. Moser is director of university housing at Florida State University.

Although little research is available on the evaluation of peer intervention programs, several strategies and approaches can be used by educators to determine the effectiveness of prejudice reduction efforts.

Evaluating Peer Interventions

Margaret A. Healy, Diane L. Cooper, Elaine C. Fygetakis

Evaluating the outcomes of prejudice reduction interventions with college students is problematic for several reasons. As Bourassa noted in Chapter Two, there are few instruments available for such evaluation and little in the research literature regarding evaluation of peer interventions for prejudice reduction purposes. Moreover, racial attitudes and values are usually firmly entrenched by the time students arrive at college, and change occurs slowly. This can make the task of evaluating change both complex and time consuming. Finally, there are many influences on students in the college environment that both reinforce and challenge racial biases and prejudices. While we want to evaluate the influences on students' attitudes or behaviors toward people of a different race, it is usually not possible to assess the impact of an isolated event or program. Attitudes and behaviors may also be influenced by living in the residence hall, taking courses, institutional policies (for example, hate speech policy), or events beyond the university environment. Such multiple influences make evaluation of interventions even more challenging as evaluators attempt to ascertain which influences are indeed present and the extent to which such influences affect outcomes. In this chapter, we examine several issues related to evaluation and suggest practical strategies for determining the effectiveness of peer interventions for prejudice reduction.

The Measurement of Change in Students' Attitudes and Behaviors

While there are few instruments that specifically measure prejudice reduction through peer interventions, there are a number of protocols that can be used to measure changes in some aspects of students' social attitudes and behaviors. One of the most frequently utilized instruments is Winston, Miller, and Prince's (1987) Student Developmental Task and Life-Style Inventory. This instrument includes a Tolerance subscale that assesses change in students' understanding of differences. While the instrument is designed to measure large shifts in student attitudes and behaviors, it can also help assess more subtle changes in levels of social bias and tolerance.

As Mann and Moser discussed in Chapter Five, another important resource for educators planning peer interventions is Helms's (1990) research on racial identity development in African Americans and whites. Helms provides an overview of a number of racial identity theories and models and proposes her own stage theory of racial identity development. This theory can help educators assess where students are with respect to racial awareness and identity and when change occurs. The Jackson and Hardiman (1988) racial identity model can be used in a similar way, as Mann and Moser discussed in Chapter Five.

Although much of Helms's (1990) work specifically addresses one-on-one relationships between counselor and client, her racial identity development theory can also be applied to other social dyads and to group interactions. Two measurement scales are particularly useful here: the Black Racial Identity Attitude Scale (Helms and Parham, 1990) and the White Racial Identity Attitude Scale (Helms and Carter, 1990). These scales can be used to assess attitudes related to various stages of racial identity development. They can also provide a foundation for planning, implementing, and subsequently evaluating peer interventions based on participants' stages of racial identity development. Utilizing the instruments in a pretest-posttest fashion helps administrators ascertain if attitudinal changes have occurred following an intervention.

Helms (1990) also provides information on self-assessment of racial identity as well as summaries of relationship types based on different combinations of race and stages of identity. The reader should refer to Helms's commentary on methodological considerations regarding the development of the scales, especially to note possible limitations and issues of validity and reliability.

Another instrument that assesses aspects of bias in attitudes and behaviors is the "People in General" portion of Stokol's (1975) Environmental Assessment Inventory. Mines (1982) also provides an overview of several other student development assessment techniques that can help evaluate general changes in students' social perspectives and personal values.

Knefelkamp and Golec (1985) offer a practical overview of the evaluation process, based on the Practice-to-Theory-to-Practice (PTP) model. Contingent on the goals of a particular program, they recommend three general evaluation strategies: (1) An evaluation of learning examines outcomes based on what information, concepts, or skills were taught to participants;

(2) an evaluation of changes in behavior, based on an experimental research design, assesses behaviors both before and after an intervention; and (3) an evaluation of satisfaction with the program measures how much the participants liked or disliked the program and its various components. All three evaluation strategies provide important measures of the effectiveness of peer intervention activities.

Loxley and Whiteley (1986) suggest three general questions that can assist the researcher in evaluating specific educational interventions: (1) Did the interventions produce changes and if so, did the changes endure? (2) Who benefited most from the intervention? Were race, gender, age, or other variables significant factors? (3) What experiences had the most impact on students? These and other questions can help the evaluator make judgments about the efficacy of an intervention and whether it needs to be modified or completely replaced.

Evaluation Methodologies

Three distinct methodologies are commonly used to determine the effectiveness of intentional educational interventions: program evaluation, experimental research, and outcomes assessment. Although these three terms are sometimes used interchangeably, there are substantial differences among them, and it is important to recognize these differences in designing evaluation strategies for peer interventions.

Program Evaluation. In program evaluation, data are collected for the purpose of making decisions about an established program's effectiveness. This method may include such activities as evaluating the success of a particular educational program or workshop, examining the service delivery of a particular department in the institution for its impact on different races and ethnic groups, or conducting a self-study of the entire institution. Program evaluation is an appropriate methodology to use when examining intact units or specific programs. This method, however, is not suitable for examining psychological or behavioral changes in individuals or for assessing complex social phenomena such as peer culture.

Program evaluation of multicultural issues in specific student service units can be accomplished using the CAS Standards and Guidelines (Council for Advancement of Standards, 1986). Educational and professional standards have been developed for most student service units and include objectives for multicultural concerns. CAS Self Assessment Guides (Miller, Thomas, Looney, and Yerian, 1988) are also available to assist in the evaluation process. Using this resource allows professionals to examine the extent to which a program or service is in compliance with the Standards.

Experimental Research. The methodology of experimental research requires a rigorous collection of data for the purpose of testing a specific hypothesis. For example, we may hypothesize that a racial attitude or behavior will change as the direct result of a particular educational intervention. Data, therefore, are collected in a systematic manner to determine whether the particular intervention is associated with a specific change. Experimental research is the method most often employed when measuring or examining changes in knowledge, values, attitudes, and behaviors on an individual level.

Suppose, for example, that one hypothesizes that students living in residence halls are not comfortable with people who are racially different from themselves. This hypothesis might be based on an observation of students in residence halls or on a theory of racial identity development such as that proposed by Jackson and Hardiman (1988) or by Helms (1990). Based on the Jackson and Hardiman model, one might further hypothesize that many student residents are at the acceptance stage of racial identity development. Individuals at this stage characteristically avoid any contact with people of other races.

An educational intervention (such as a program, a flier, or a series of activities) can then be initiated with the goal of increasing interaction and tolerance. In order to determine if the educational intervention promotes a change in students' comfort level with students of other races in the residence hall, one could measure their comfort level before beginning the program using a survey (see Figure 6.1) based on social distance theory (Robinson, 1987). After the educational intervention has been completed, the social distance survey could be readministered. Any change in scores could then be examined, both for individuals and for the residence hall as a living unit.

Outcomes Assessment. The third methodology is designed to measure whether a predetermined outcome has been achieved as the result of an intentional intervention. Outcome measures are often defined as values or goals for a department or institution, and data can be both qualitative and quantitative. For example, if a student activities office has a goal of increasing the interaction among students of different races, that outcome could be assessed in several ways. It could be measured qualitatively by observing student interactions at events sponsored by the student activities office, and a simple quantitative measure, such as counting the number of white students and students of color who attend various types of student activity programs, could also be used to document participation levels.

Another example of outcomes assessment is the review of resident assistants' (RAs') incident reports for the year. Such a review might reveal that students of color and international students are overrepresented among those accused of misconduct or problem behaviors in the hall. Such a review might also suggest that the incident reports are greatly influenced by RAs' difficulty in dealing with residents and guests who are of a different race than themselves. Based on this assessment, an intervention can be

Figure 6.1. Measure of Social Distance

SOCIAL ATTITUDE

Using the following scale, please assign the whole number (1–7) that best describes the closest relationship you would be willing to have with each group below. The numbers form a continuous scale from the closest relationship (1 = marry) to the furthest relationship (7 = exclude). Make sure that your reactions are to each group as a whole, not to the best or worst members you may have known.

1. Would *marry* or allow family member to marry
2. Would have as a good *friend*
3. Would have as my *neighbor*
4. Would have in the same *work* group
5. Would have as a speaking *acquaintance* only
6. Would have as a *visitor* to my country only
7. Would *exclude* from my country

marry	friend	neighbor	co-worker	acquaintance	visitor	exclude
1	2	3	4	5	6	7

a. _____ Whites

b. _____ African Americans

c. _____ Hispanic Americans

d. _____ American Indians

e. _____ Internationals

f. _____ Orientals

g. _____ Arabs

h. _____ Africans

i. _____ Indians (from India)

j. _____ Europeans

k. _____ South/Central Americans

l. _____ Russians

m. _____ Iranians

n. _____ South Africans (blacks)

o. _____ South Africans (whites)

p. _____ Nicaraguans

q. _____ Homosexuals

r. _____ Drug users

s. _____ Drinkers

t. _____ Nondrinkers

u. _____ Smokers

v. _____ Nonsmokers

w. _____ Christians

x. _____ Born-again Christians

y. _____ Jews

z. _____ Muslims

aa. _____ Fraternity/sorority members

bb. _____ Students from rural areas

cc. _____ Students from large urban areas

dd. _____ Football players

ee. _____ Basketball players

ff. _____ Wrestlers

gg. _____ Swimmers

hh. _____ Gymnasts

ii. _____ Track/field athletes

jj. _____ Tennis players

Source: Quality of Life Survey, Department of Residence Life, Iowa State University (Robinson, 1987). Used with permission.

designed to enhance the ability of RAs to communicate and work more effectively with peers from different racial or ethnic groups.

The three evaluation methodologies discussed here are all useful in assessing the impact of peer interventions, but they differ significantly in purpose and operation. These differences need to be weighed by the educator in designing evaluation strategies.

A Sample Program Evaluation

To illustrate a practical approach to evaluation, we will consider how we might evaluate an educational program designed to increase understanding and awareness of African American students by white student members of an all-campus student programming board and to increase the racial diversity of programs and activities sponsored by the board.

The program intervention could be as simple as bringing together the white student members of the programming board with members of the campus's black student union (BSU) to examine differences in programming interests and personal attitudes and values. The goals of such an intervention may be to encourage white student leaders to develop closer personal contact and interaction with African American students; to assist white students in working through the resistance stage and into the redefinition stage (Jackson and Hardiman, 1988) in order to promote the development of an affirming social identity, and to increase the number of African American performers and presenters on campus throughout the entire year.

The first two goals of the intervention could be evaluated through structured interviews with each of the white students involved. In preparation for the interviews, these students might be asked to keep a journal whose entries respond to a list of specific questions regarding the white students' interaction with African American students and their mutual programming efforts. The students could also be asked to record other recent situations (besides the intervention) that they believe have affected their attitudes toward people of different races. Such probing can help to ascertain if other environmental factors may have contributed to individual changes. Last but not least, student activities staff could be surveyed at the end of the academic year to note the number of African Americans brought to campus through sponsored and cosponsored events.

Always keep in mind that evaluations should help you measure changes that can be attributed to the intervention itself. Evaluation methods should usually measure both behavioral and attitudinal changes. In our example, the evaluator may decide to develop different means to ascertain behavioral changes. For instance, one could note how frequently white student programmers include BSU ideas in their meeting agendas or program planning. It could then be determined how many of these ideas are actually carried through to completion. What is the nature of these ideas, which students are spearheading the efforts, and are white and African American students working collaboratively? Indeed, are the programs brought about through collaborative efforts or simply through the efforts of one or two students of a particular race? Have students asked to become active members in the BSU or the programming board, going beyond the requirement simply to attend the other group's meetings as a representative of their own group? All of these questions can help ascertain if behavioral changes have taken place. The information can be gathered through the evaluator's observations based on clearly defined criteria. Additional criteria may be added if unanticipated behavior patterns emerge during the observation process. Similar strategies can be used when attempting to measure a change in the attitudes and behaviors of any student group.

Others should also be trained to assist in the observation process. After the evaluator explains what types of behaviors to look for, two raters (one might be the primary researcher) can observe a particular meeting. The researcher can then compare how the two raters have evaluated the same situation. This process helps to address interrater or intercoder reliability. Ideally, the two observers would rate all or most of what they have observed in the same way. Well-defined criteria and specially trained raters can add credence to the intervention and its subsequent evaluation. Multiple raters can also help the researcher recognize when criteria (in this case, those encompassing actual behaviors) have not been clearly defined.

When using such methods as structured interviews, journals, and questionnaires to measure attitudinal change, evaluators should clearly define criteria prior to the evaluation process. Students can be asked to describe if and how their attitudes have changed because of the intervention (or other environmental factors). One can also administer an "attitudes" questionnaire prior to the intervention. Questions can address the individual's attitudes toward students of different races and the attitudes of student organizations (such as the BSU and the programming board) that are traditionally racially homogeneous. After the intervention has taken its course (in this case, after about a year's time), the questionnaire can be readministered to students who completed the first one. The evaluator can then compare their attitudes prior to and following the intervention. Multiple raters or observers can again be utilized in this process. If appropriate, criteria can be redefined to include any emerging patterns of attitudinal change. Since attitudinal change—just like behavioral change—occurs over time, it would be ideal to collect data again at some later point after the initial evaluation.

It is not necessary to collect behavioral and attitudinal data separately. Similarly, student affairs professionals are encouraged to use both quantitative and qualitative methods to evaluate the intervention. Since attitudes and values change slowly, longitudinal research is best. Recognize that the evaluation will usually help one understand relationships among criteria or variables rather than attribute cause and effect.

It is obvious that many practitioners do not have the time or the resources to conduct interventions based on strict research paradigms. But a thoughtful research design—preferably based on a theoretical framework with a clear understanding of the factors to be examined—can help ensure that an intervention is appropriate and that it can be evaluated effectively.

References

Council for the Advancement of Standards for Student Services/Development Programs. *CAS Standards for Student Services/Development Programs.* Washington, D.C.: Council for the Advancement of Standards for Student Services/Development Programs, 1986.

Helms, J. E. (ed.). *Black and White Racial Identity: Theory, Research, and Practice.* New York: Greenwood Press, 1990.

Helms, J. E., and Carter, R. T. "White Racial Identity Attitude Scale." In J. E. Helms (ed.), *Black and White Racial Identity: Theory, Research, and Practice.* New York: Greenwood Press, 1990.

Helms, J. E., and Parham, T. A. "Black Racial Identity Attitude Scale." In J. E. Helms (ed.), *Black and White Racial Identity: Theory, Research, and Practice.* New York: Greenwood Press, 1990.

Jackson, B. W., and Hardiman, R. "Oppression: Conceptual and Developmental Analysis." In M. Adams and L. Marchesani (eds.), *Racial and Cultural Diversity, Curricular Content, and Classroom Dynamics: A Manual for College Teachers.* Amherst: University of Massachusetts, 1988.

Knefelkamp, L. L., and Golec, R. R. *A Workbook for Using the PTP Model.* College Park: University of Maryland, 1985.

Loxley, J. C., and Whiteley, J. M. *Character Development in College Students.* Vol. 2. Schenectady, N.Y.: Character Research Press, 1986.

Miller, T. K., Thomas, W. L., Looney, S. C., and Yenan, J. *CAS Self Assessment Guides.* Washington, D.C.: Council for the Advancement of Standards for Student Services/Development Programs, 1986.

Mines, R. A. "Student Development Assessment Techniques." In G. R. Hanson (ed.), *Measuring Student Development.* New Directions for Student Services, no. 20. San Francisco: Jossey-Bass, 1982.

Robinson, P. J. "The Relationship Between Favorable or Unfavorable Contact on the Social Distance Attitudes of Residence Hall Students Toward Residential Subgroups." Unpublished doctoral dissertation, Iowa State University, 1987.

Stokol, D. "Toward a Psychological Theory of Alienation." *Psychological Review,* 1975, 82 (1), 26-44.

Winston, R. B., Jr., Miller, T. K., and Prince, J. S. *Student Developmental Task and Life-Style Inventory.* Athens, Ga.: Student Development Associates, 1987.

Margaret A. Healy is assistant vice chancellor for student affairs at the University of North Carolina at Greensboro.

Diane L. Cooper is assistant to the vice chancellor for student affairs at the University of North Carolina at Greensboro.

Elaine C. Fygetakis is a doctoral candidate in higher education administration at Florida State University.

This chapter contains information about resources that may be valuable for those working to understand and counteract racism on college campuses. The references at the end of each chapter provide other useful resources.

Resources

Roberta Christie, Renée Borns

Please refer to the References at the end of each chapter for other valuable resources.

Books and Monographs

Ashley, M. E. *Combating Racism on Campus: A Resource Book and Model for the 1990s.* Cincinnati, Ohio: University of Cincinnati, 1990.

The author advocates that the following actions must be taken to combat racism on campus: (1) Demonstrate institution-wide commitment. (2) Increase the hiring and professional development of minority faculty and staff. (3) Increase access and academic support systems for minority students. (4) Infuse the campus climate with a value on diversity. (5) Require training for all in the understanding of other cultures. (6) Develop a multicultural curriculum. (7) Strengthen local community linkages. (8) Devise intervention strategies. (9) Demand accountability. The author discusses measuring program effectiveness and offers brief descriptions of applications of models at the University of Wisconsin (Madison and Milwaukee), University of Michigan, University of Louisville, and University of Cincinnati. A short annotated bibliography and an extensive bibliography of references and further readings are included.

Ehrlich, H. J. *Campus Ethnoviolence and the Policy Options.* Baltimore, Md.: National Institute Against Prejudice and Violence, 1990.

This concise report of the National Institute Against Prejudice and Violence includes a brief history of ethnoviolence, its societal and college campus contexts, and strategies for preventing and responding to incidents. References to case studies and abstracts of selected incidents of conflict and ethnoviolence on college campuses from 1986 through 1988 are included.

Green, M. (ed.). *Minorities on Campus: A Handbook for Enhancing Diversity.* Washington, D.C.: American Council on Education, 1989.

This handbook proposes strategies to reverse the trend of declining participation by people of color in higher education. It contains an overview of the status of minorities, descriptions of mechanisms to use in auditing minority participation, recruiting and retention strategies, information on interactions between teachers and students, strategies for designing curriculum to attract minorities, and ways to create a welcoming campus climate.

Helms, J. E. (ed.). *Black and White Racial Identity: Theory, Research, and Practice.* New York: Greenwood Press, 1990.

This book details Helms's stage theory on racial identity development in African Americans and whites. Written from a counseling psychology perspective, the book offers a practical framework and several instruments that can be used by educators as well as counselors.

Hively, R. (ed.). *The Lurking Evil: Racial and Ethnic Conflict on the College Campus.* Washington, D.C.: American Association of State Colleges and Universities, 1990.

This publication was prompted by a meeting of university presidents at the White House in October 1989. The sixteen essays offer information that can serve higher education administrators in appraising and solving the problems that may arise from racial and ethnic tensions on their campuses.

Hustopes, T., and Connolly, W., Jr. (eds.). *Regulating Racial Harassment on Campus: A Legal Compendium.* Washington, D.C.: National Association of College and University Attorneys, 1990.

The editors offer materials related to the University of Michigan antiharassment policy and challenges to it, other sample racial harassment policies or policy drafts adopted or proposed by other universities, and selected articles and commentary.

Moses, Y. T. *Black Women in Academe: Issues and Strategies.* Washington, D.C.: Project on the Status and Education of Women, Association of American Colleges, 1989.

This report examines the impact of racism and sexism on African American women in academia. The report succinctly treats such issues as admissions and financial aid, choice of study, curricula, residential and social life, sexuality and sexual harassment, retention, research, teaching, and tenure. It includes recommendations for action, selected references, and a list of research and resource centers.

Sedlacek, W. E., and Brooks, G. C., Jr. *Racism in American Education: A Model for Change*. Chicago: Welson-Hall, 1976.
The authors describe a systematic and pragmatic approach to confronting racism. They discuss (with frequent references to research) cultural and racial differences and how racism operates, they examine racial attitudes and their sources, and they address how behavior can be changed.

Journals and Magazines

Black Issues in Higher Education—Biweekly; $25 for first year, $40 for renewals. (Cox, Matthews, and Associates, Inc., 1520 Warwick Avenue, Suite B-8, Fairfax, VA 22030; telephone: 703-385-2981.)

Black Collegiate—Quarterly; $10 a year. (Black Collegiate Services, Inc., 1240 South Broad Avenue, New Orleans, LA 70125; telephone: 504-821-5694.)

Newsletters

The *Law Report of the Southern Poverty Law Center* is devoted to organizational activities and victories in the struggle for racial equality. ($15 contribution or more; Southern Poverty Law Center, 400 Washington Avenue, P.O. Box 548, Montgomery, AL 36101-0548; telephone: 205-264-0286.)

The *Monitor of the Center for Democratic Renewal* monitors manifestations of racism and efforts to combat it. ($15 individuals, $25 institutions; Center for Democratic Renewal, P.O. Box 50469, Atlanta, GA 30302; telephone: 404-221-0025.)

Progressive Student News is published by the Progressive Student Network, a student-run organization devoted to linking college student activism on issues including racism and sexism. ($6; Progressive Student News, Box 1027, Iowa City, IA 52244.)

UC RAPPS shares perspectives and information about campus programs committed to racial awareness and diversity in higher education. (Racial Awareness Pilot Project Office, 404 Dabney Hall M.L. 45, University of Cincinnati, Cincinnati, OH 45221; telephone: 513-556-5251.)

The *Web*, published by the American Indian Program at Cornell University, reports primarily on academic and educational issues affecting Native Americans and on organization activities. (Free; American Indian Program, 300 Caldwell Hall, Cornell University, Ithaca, NY 14853; telephone: 607-255-6587.)

The *WREE View of Women* is the newsletter of the Women for Racial and Economic Equality, an organization that seeks economic security for women and the elimination of racism. International in scope, the newsletter provides a forum for global discussion of the issues. ($7 low-income, $20 regular, $50 sustaining; Women for Racial and Economic Equality, 198 Broadway, Room 606, New York, NY 10038; telephone: 212-385-1103.)

Videotapes

"Black by Popular Demand"—Created by an Iowa State University student, this video calls attention to the academic, financial, and social aspects of being African American on a predominantly white campus. (30 minutes; $189 purchase, $99 rental; Thomas Furgerson, Redshoes Productions, P.O. Box 1793, Des Moines, IA 50306; telephone: 515-292-1883.)

"Eyes on the Prize" and "Eyes on the Prize II"—These two highly acclaimed series focus on the people, events, and issues of the civil rights struggle in the U.S. from 1954–1965 and 1965–1985. They provide a thorough and moving history in which dramatic moments come to life through archival footage and interviews. (Series I: six hour-long programs, $295; Series II: eight hour-long programs, $395; purchase only; PBS Video, 1320 Braddock Place, Alexandria, VA 22314; telephone: 800-424-7963.)

"Facing Difference: Living Together on Campus"—This videotape and leader's guide addresses typical incidents of public expression and overt acts of prejudice on college campuses. Racial, religious, ethnic, and sexual orientation diversities are explored. The program is designed for use during new-student orientation. (11 minutes; $90 purchase; Anti-Defamation League, 823 United National Plaza, New York, NY 10017; telephone: 212-490-2525.)

"Minorities in the Classroom: Racism in Education"—Produced by Michigan State University, this tape features vignettes demonstrating how professors exhibit racial prejudice in the classroom. (26 minutes; $300 purchase, $200 rental; Ralph Bonner, Department of Human Relations, Michigan State University, East Lansing, MI 48824-1046; telephone: 517-353-3922.)

"Still Burning: Confronting Ethnoviolence on Campus"—These two videotapes describe the University of Maryland's policies and procedures for handling incidents of ethnoviolence on campus. In Part Two, students of color speak of their experiences and the need for administrative action. (Part I: 17

minutes; Part II: 21 minutes; $120 for both; Instructional Media Resources, University of Maryland, Baltimore County, Catonsville, MD 21228; telephone: 301-455-3208.)

Organizations, Institutes, and Consultants

The Anti-Defamation League of B'nai B'rith monitors campus racism and bias and provides consultation and materials. (823 United Nations Plaza, New York, NY 10017; telephone: 212-490-2525.)

The Campus Violence Prevention Center maintains a data base on campus violence and its causes. Staff seek to build awareness about the extent, scope, and impact of campus violence and to serve as a networking center for all interested in research and information on the topic. (Student Services Division, Towson State University, Towson, MD 21204; telephone: 301-830-2178.)

The Institute for Multicultural Education and Training sponsors institutes and conferences. (Lenoir-Rhyne College, Hickory, NC 28603; telephone: 704-328-7353.)

The Martin Luther King, Jr., Center for Nonviolent Social Change offers workshops on nonviolence, coalition building, and conflict resolution. (449 Auburn Avenue NE, Atlanta, GA 30312; telephone: 404-524-1956.)

The National Council of La Raza monitors and issues reports on Hispanics in the U.S. (810 First Street NE, Washington, D.C. 20002; telephone: 202-289-1380.)

The National Institute Against Prejudice and Violence is a clearinghouse that monitors racism in the United States. (31 South Greene Street, Baltimore, MD 21201; telephone: 301-328-5170.)

The Student Coalition Against Apartheid and Racism works against South African apartheid and domestic racism and aims to increase the number of minority and women faculty members and to help historically and predominantly black institutions and ethnic studies programs survive. (P.O. Box 18291, Washington, D.C. 20036; telephone: 202-483-4593.)

The Women Against Racism Committee is a "working laboratory" that offers workshops on combating racism and on ways to build coalitions. (Ms. Papusa Nolina, Women's Resource and Action Center, University of Iowa, 130 North Madison Street, Iowa City, IA 52240; telephone: 319-335-1486.)

Conferences

The International Society for Intercultural Education, Training, and Research (SIETAR International) is a professional service organization providing annual conferences that focus on promoting effective communication and cooperative interaction among people of diverse cultures and ethnic groups. (SIETAR International, 733 15th Street NW, Suite 900, Washington, D.C. 20005; telephone: 202-737-5000.)

The National Conference on Racial and Ethnic Relations in American Higher Education is sponsored annually by the Southwest Center for Human Relations Studies, Continuing Education and Public Service, University of Oklahoma. (555 Constitution, Norman, OK 73037-0005; telephone: 405-325-3936.)

The Summer Institute for Intercultural Communication is a yearly conference, workshop, and internship program devoted to intercultural training and education. (Janet Bennett or Milton Bennett, 8835 Canyon Lane SW, Suite 238, Portland, OR 97225; telephone: 503-297-4622.)

Programs and Activities

Awards/Recognition
InView, a college women's magazine, grants an award for an outstanding contribution to interracial harmony and understanding. (*InView*, Whittle Communications, 529 Fifth Avenue, 11th Floor, New York, NY 10017; telephone: 212-916-3300.)

Peer Mentoring
Peer facilitators for African American, Hispanic, Jewish, American Indian, gay and lesbian, and disabled students provide support for their counterparts at Florida State University. Facilitators receive twenty hours of training in peer consultation and are supervised by counselors. (Delories Sloan, Thagard Student Health Center, Florida State University, Tallahassee, FL 32306; telephone: 904-644-2003.)

Policies
Pennsylvania State University includes racial incidents and other "acts of intolerance" as violations in its policies and rules for students. Special attention is given in these policies to ensuring fair hearings following racial incidents. (Pat Peterson, Assistant Vice President for Student Services, 135 Boucke Building, University Park, PA 16802; telephone: 814-863-1809.)

The University of Michigan, Ann Arbor, instituted a Discrimination Act Policy. In 1989–90, 113 complaints were reported. (Roselle Wilson, Assistant Vice President for Student Services, Michigan Union, University of Michigan, Ann Arbor, MI 48109-1314; telephone: 313-764-7420.)

Raising Awareness
Advocates for National Greek Leadership and Education (ANGLE) is an organization that trains peer educators to work in Greek chapters on alcohol and drug use, date rape, and cultural diversity issues. The network office provides educational materials and ideas. (Ron Butler, Student Activities Office, University of California, Irvine, CA 92717; telephone: 714-856-5182.)

Greeks for Racial and Cultural Education (GRACE) is a peer education program that addresses issues of diversity by educating Greek leaders and the larger community at the University of California, Santa Barbara. (Patrick Naessens, Greek Affairs Adviser, University of California, Santa Barbara, CA 93106; telephone: 805-893-4553.)

Racial Awareness Pilot Project (RAPP) brings together twenty-five culturally diverse students to share personal feelings about racial issues. Selected by application, students spend five to ten hours weekly in RAPP discussions and educational programs. Veteran "RAPPers" assist the RAPP group and sponsor programs. (Linda Bates-Parker, Career Dynamics Center, ML 115, University of Cincinnati, OH 45221; telephone: 513-556-3471.)

The Racism Improvisational Group performs vignettes illustrating subtle acts of racism and then leads group discussions. (Camille Clay, Assistant Vice President for Student Affairs, Towson State University, Towson, MD 21204; telephone: 301-830-2051.)

Students in the Division of Theater and Arts at the State University of New York College, Purchase, produced *Under the Skin,* a play about stereotypes that fuel racism, anti-Semitism, sexism, homophobia, and other forms of discrimination. (Israel Hicks, SUNY College, Purchase, NY 10577; telephone: 914-251-6831.)

The Education Program to Increase Racial Awareness at the University of California, Santa Barbara (UCSB), produced "To Be a Black Student at UCSB," a videotape of interviews with dozens of African American students. Shown to students, faculty, and staff, the video serves as a basis for discussion and learning. (Director, Education Program to Increase Racial Awareness, University of California, Santa Barbara, CA 93106; telephone: 805-893-8386.)

Using grant money from the Fund for the Improvement of Postsecondary Education, the University of Tennessee, Knoxville, produced videotapes to improve race relations in the classroom. (Camille Hazear, Director of Affirmative Action Programming, University of Tennessee, 403C Andy Holt Tower, Knoxville, TN 37996-0144; telephone: 615-974-2498.)

Reporting
The brochure, *Racism—Let Us Know,* urges University of Wisconsin, Madison, students to report incidents of racism. The university promises to preserve confidentiality and to take no official action without the consent of the victim. (Mary Rouse, Dean of Students, University of Wisconsin, 109 Bascom Hall, Madison, WI 53706; telephone: 608-363-5700.)

A twenty-four-hour hot line for reporting incidents of harassment and discrimination serves the University of Kansas. (Robert Shelton, Director, Ombudsman's Program, 104 Smith Hall, Lawrence, KS 66045; telephone: 913-864-4665.)

Reacting to Racism
State University of New York officials send "hit squads" to racially troubled campuses to improve the racial climate and to suggest administrative action. (Frank Pogue, Jr., Vice Chancellor for Student Affairs and Special Programs, SUNY Central Administration, State University Plaza, Albany, NY 12246; telephone: 518-443-5137.)

Renée Borns is completing her master's in higher education administration at Florida State University.

Roberta Christie is director of student affairs research and assessment at Florida State University.

INDEX

ORDERING INFORMATION

NEW DIRECTIONS FOR STUDENT SERVICES is a series of paperback books that offers guidelines and programs for aiding students in their total development—emotional, social, and physical, as well as intellectual. Books in the series are published quarterly in Fall, Winter, Spring, and Summer and are available for purchase by subscription as well as by single copy.

SUBSCRIPTIONS for 1991 cost $45.00 for individuals (a savings of 20 percent over single-copy prices) and $60.00 for institutions, agencies, and libraries. Please do not send institutional checks for personal subscriptions. Standing orders are accepted.

SINGLE COPIES cost $14.95 when payment accompanies order. (California, New Jersey, New York, and Washington, D.C., residents please include appropriate sales tax.) Billed orders will be charged postage and handling.

DISCOUNTS FOR QUANTITY ORDERS are available. Please write to the address below for information.

ALL ORDERS must include either the name of an individual or an official purchase order number. Please submit your order as follows:
  Subscriptions: specify series and year subscription is to begin
  Single copies: include individual title code (such as SS1)

MAIL ALL ORDERS TO:
  Jossey-Bass Inc., Publishers
  350 Sansome Street
  San Francisco, California 94104

FOR SALES OUTSIDE OF THE UNITED STATES CONTACT:
  Maxwell Macmillan International Publishing Group
  866 Third Avenue
  New York, New York 10022

1A. Title of Publication		1B. PUBLICATION NO.							2. Date of Filing
New Directions for Student Services		4	4	9	-	0	7	0	10/11/91

3. Frequency of Issue	3A. No. of Issues Published Annually	3B. Annual Subscription Price
Quarterly	Four (4)	$45 (individual) $60 (institutional)

4. Complete Mailing Address of Known Office of Publication (Street, City, County, State and ZIP+4 Code) (Not printers)
350 Sansome Street, San Francisco, CA 94104-1310

5. Complete Mailing Address of the Headquarters of General Business Offices of the Publisher (Not printer)
(above address)

6. Full Names and Complete Mailing Address of Publisher, Editor, and Managing Editor (This item MUST NOT be blank)

Publisher (Name and Complete Mailing Address)
Jossey-Bass Inc., Publishers (above address)

Editor (Name and Complete Mailing Address)
Margaret J. Barr, Sadler Hall, Texas Christian University, Fort Worth, TX 76129

Managing Editor (Name and Complete Mailing Address)
Lynn Luckow, President, Jossey-Bass Inc., Publishers (above address)

7. Owner (If owned by a corporation, its name and address must be stated and also immediately thereunder the names and addresses of stockholders owning or holding 1 percent or more of total amount of stock. If not owned by a corporation, the names and addresses of the individual owners must be given. If owned by a partnership or other unincorporated firm, its name and address, as well as that of each individual must be given. If the publication is published by a nonprofit organization, its name and address must be stated.) (Item must be completed.)

Full Name	Complete Mailing Address
Maxwell Communications Corp., plc	Headington Hill Hall Oxford OX30BW U.K.

8. Known Bondholders, Mortgagees, and Other Security Holders Owning or Holding 1 Percent or More of Total Amount of Bonds, Mortgages or Other Securities (If there are none, so state)

Full Name	Complete Mailing Address
name as above	name as above

9. For Completion by Nonprofit Organizations Authorized To Mail at Special Rates (DMM Section 423.12 only)
The purpose, function, and nonprofit status of this organization and the exempt status for Federal income tax purposes (Check one)

(1) ☐ Has Not Changed During Preceding 12 Months	(2) ☐ Has Changed During Preceding 12 Months	(If changed, publisher must submit explanation of change with this statement.)

10. Extent and Nature of Circulation (See instructions on reverse side)	Average No. Copies Each Issue During Preceding 12 Months	Actual No. Copies of Single Issue Published Nearest to Filing Date
A. Total No. Copies (Net Press Run)	2100	2206
B. Paid and/or Requested Circulation 1. Sales through dealers and carriers, street vendors and counter sales	136	28
2. Mail Subscription (Paid and/or requested)	988	1080
C. Total Paid and/or Requested Circulation (Sum of 10B1 and 10B2)	1124	1108
D. Free Distribution by Mail, Carrier or Other Means Samples, Complimentary, and Other Free Copies	120	86
E. Total Distribution (Sum of C and D)	1244	1194
F. Copies Not Distributed 1. Office use, left over, unaccounted, spoiled after printing	856	1012
2. Return from News Agents	-0-	-0-
G. TOTAL (Sum of E, F1 and 2—should equal net press run shown in A)	2100	2206

11. I certify that the statements made by me above are correct and complete	Signature and Title of Editor, Publisher, Business Manager, or Owner *[signature]*	Lorry Iobii Vice-President

PS Form **3526**, Feb. 1989   (See instructions on reverse)